The Wadsworth Casebook
for Reading, Research, and Writing

Trifles
Susan Glaspell

Contributing Editor

Donna Winchell
Clemson University

Series Editors

Laurie G. Kirszner
University of the Sciences in Philadelphia

Stephen R. Mandell
Drexel University

THOMSON
WADSWORTH

Australia Canada Mexico Singapore Spain United Kingdom United States

The Wadsworth Casebook Series for Reading, Research, and Writing
Susan Glaspell, *Trifles*

Publisher: *Michael Rosenberg*
Senior Editor: *Aron Keesbury*
Developmental Editor: *Marita Sermolins*
Production Editor: *Samantha Ross*
Marketing Manager: *Carrie Brandon*
Senior Print Buyer: *Mary Beth Hennebury*
Compositor: *Publishers' Design and Production Services*
Photography Manager: *Sheri Blaney*
Cover/Text Designer: *Linda Beaupré*
Printer: *West Group*

Cover Image: © *Linda Beaupré/Stone House Art*

Printed in the United States of America.
2 3 4 5 6 7 8 9 10   07 06

For more information contact Wadsworth, 25 Thomson Place, Boston, MA 02210 USA, or you can visit our Internet site at http://www.wadsworth.com

ISBN: 1-4130-0045-2

Library of Congress Control Number: 2003110792

About the Series

The Wadsworth Casebook Series for Reading, Research, and Writing has its origins in our anthology *Literature: Reading, Reacting, Writing* (Fifth Edition, 2004), which in turn arose out of our many years of teaching college writing and literature courses. The primary purpose of each Casebook in the series is to offer students a convenient, self-contained reference tool that they can use to gain insight into a work (or works) of literature and to complete a research project for an introductory literature course.

In choosing subjects for the Casebooks, we drew on our own experience in the classroom, selecting works of poetry, fiction, and drama that students like to read, discuss, and write about and that teachers like to teach. Unlike other collections of literary criticism aimed at students, the Wadsworth Casebook Series for Reading, Research, and Writing features short stories, groups of poems, or plays (rather than longer works, such as novels) because these are the genres most often taught in college-level Introduction to Literature courses. In selecting particular authors and titles, we focus on those most frequently assigned and those most accessible to students.

To facilitate student research — and to facilitate instructor supervision of that research — each Casebook contains all the resources students need to produce a documented research paper on a particular work of literature. Every Casebook in the series includes the following elements:

- A comprehensive **introduction** to the work, providing a social, historical, and political background. This introduction helps students to understand the work and the author in the context of a particular time and place. In particular, the introduction enables students to appreciate customs, events, and ideas that may have contributed to the author's choice of subject matter, emphasis, or style.

- **About the Author,** a biographical discussion that includes information such as the author's birth and death dates; details of the work's first publication and its subsequent publication history, if relevant; details about the author's life; a summary of the author's career; and a discussion of key published works.

- The most widely accepted version of the **literary work,** along with the explanatory footnotes students will need to understand unfamiliar terms and concepts or references to people, places, or events.

- **Discussion questions** focusing on themes developed in the work. These questions, designed to stimulate critical thinking and discussion, can also serve as springboards for research projects.

- A list of topics for extended **research assignments** related to the literary work. Students may use these assignments exactly as they appear in the Casebook, or students or instructors may modify the assignments to suit their own needs or research interests.

- A diverse collection of traditional and nontraditional **secondary sources,** which may include scholarly articles, reviews, interviews, memoirs, newspaper articles, historical documents, and so on, as well as photographs and other visuals. This resource offers students access to sources they might not turn to on their own — for example, a popular song that inspired a short story, a story that was the original version of a play, a legal document that sheds light on a work's theme, or two different biographies of an author — thus encouraging students to look beyond the obvious or the familiar as they search for ideas. Students may use only these sources, or they may supplement them with sources listed in the Casebook's bibliography (see below).

- An annotated model **student research paper** drawing on several of the Casebook's secondary sources. This paper uses MLA parenthetical documentation and includes a Works Cited list conforming to MLA style.

- A comprehensive **bibliography** of print and electronic sources related to the work. This bibliography offers students an opportunity to move beyond the sources in the Casebook to other sources related to a particular research topic.

- A concise, up-to-date **guide to MLA documentation,** including information on what kinds of information require documentation (and what kinds do not); a full explanation of how to construct parenthetical references and how to place them in a paper; sample parenthetical reference formats for various kinds of sources used in papers about literature; a complete explanation of how to assemble a works-cited list accompanied by sample works-cited entries (including formats for documenting electronic sources); and guidelines for using explanatory notes (with examples).

By collecting all this essential information in one convenient place, each volume in the Wadsworth Casebook Series for Reading, Research, and Writing responds to the needs of both students and teachers. For students, the Casebooks offer convenience, referentiality, and portability, making the process of doing research easier. For instructors, the Casebooks offer the flexibility and control necessary to teach students how to use sources when writing about literature. For example, teachers may choose to assign one Casebook or more than one; thus, they have the option of having all students in a class write about the same work or having different groups of students, or individual students, write about different works. In addition, instructors may ask students to use only the secondary sources collected in the Casebook, thereby controlling students' use of (and acknowledgment of) sources more closely, or they may encourage students to seek sources (both print and electronic) beyond those included in the Casebook. By building convenience, structure, and flexibility into each volume, we have designed the Wadsworth Casebook Series for Reading, Research, and Writing to suit a wide variety of teaching styles and research interests. The Casebooks have made the research paper an easier project for us and a less stressful one for our students; we hope they will do the same for you.

Laurie G. Kirszner
Stephen R. Mandell
Series Editors

Preface

The play *Trifles* is the single work on which Susan Glaspell's current fame primarily rests. Although the one-act play, first performed in 1916 and first published in 1920, appears in numerous anthologies of American literature, many readers are probably unaware that Glaspell was a Pulitzer Prize–winning dramatist, having won the prestigious award in 1931 for *Alison's House*, or that she played a leading role in the history of American drama.

In 1915, Glaspell and her husband George Cram Cook converted an old fishhouse across from their summer home in Provincetown, Massachusetts, into a makeshift theater in which to put on plays to entertain other intellectuals who, like themselves, came to Provincetown to escape the summer heat. The success of their first season led Cook to promise a new play by his wife for the next bill. In her biography of her husband, Glaspell makes clear that she took up an unfamiliar literary form in order to please him. Up to that point she had written short stories and novels. As she sat and stared at the fishhouse, waiting for inspiration, she saw taking shape a scene from her former career as a reporter in her hometown of Davenport, Iowa. The basic outline of a homicide about which she had written news stories thus became the subject matter for her best-known work, and her first dramatic endeavor took up a theme that would resonate through most of her work. A woman accused of murdering her husband in early twentieth-century Iowa had no hope of being judged by other women in a court of law. In *Trifles*, two women take on the roles of judge and jury as they visit the kitchen of the accused and there discover bits of evidence that provide the motivation for the murder, bits of evidence to "trifling" and too much the world of women to deserve notice by men.

The true story on which *Trifles* is based seems to have captured and held Glaspell's attention. She returned to it in 1917 when she transformed her play into the short story "A Jury of Her Peers."

This casebook provides a sampling of some of the best research and critical work that has been done on the play since feminist critics drew renewed attention to it during the last decades of the twentieth century.

The first of the secondary sources included is Linda Ben-Zvi's detailed account of the historical source on which the play was based and of Glaspell's relationship to the case. The next three pieces, by Alkalay-Gut, Mael, and Stein, provide different feminist readings of the play and of the time during which it was written and performed. The final two sources are Glaspell's own short story "A Jury of Her Peers" and an analysis by Mustazza of the changes that occurred as the play was transformed into a short story.

- Ben-Zvi, Linda. From " 'Murder, She Wrote': The Genesis of Susan Glaspell's *Trifles*." Ben-Zvi provides a detailed account of the historical source upon which *Trifles* is based—a murder in Iowa in 1900—and used the news accounts that Glaspell filed to show her artistic evolution and the cultural shifts between 1900 and the year the play was written, 1916.

- Alkalay-Gut, Karen. "Murder and Marriage: Another Look at *Trifles*." Alkalay-Gut analyzes the double bind in which women of the early twentieth century found themselves, in danger from a legal system in which they were denied a part and also from the structure of marriage itself.

- Mael, Phyllis. "*Trifles*: The Path to Sisterhood." Mael examines the play in light of current feminist research in developmental psychology and Sally Heckel's 1981 film adaptation of the work, examining Heckel's use of visual effects to highlight each "trifle" and to reinforce relationships.

- Stein, Karen F. "The Women's World of Glaspell's *Trifles*." Stein examines *Trifles* as an anomaly in the murder mystery genre, in which solving the mystery of John Wright's death becomes a cooperative and feminist endeavor.

- Glaspell, Susan. "A Jury of Her Peers." The short story that evolved in 1917 from the play.

- Mustazza, Leonard. "Generic Translation and Thematic Shift in Susan Glaspell's *Trifles* and 'A Jury of Her Peers.'" Mustazza examines how in making the transition from play to short story Glaspell adds depth to the relationships among the play's female characters.

Following the play are discussion questions and research topics presented as aids to thinking and writing about *Trifles* and related sources. After the secondary sources comes a student essay by Kelli Bolt that makes use of several of the secondary sources in interpreting the play and illustrates the proper use of MLA style to document sources from this casebook.

ACKNOWLEDGMENTS

I wish to thank Laurie G. Kirszner and Stephen R. Mandell, the Wadsworth Casebook Series for Reading, Research, and Writing series editors, and others at Heinle who have helped bring this project to fruition: Aron Keesbury, Senior Developmental Editor; Marita Sermolins, Editorial Assistant in English; and Michell Phifer, longtime friend. I owe a special debt of gratitude to Kelli Bolt, the author of the sample student essay, who helped me tremendously in locating and documenting information about Glaspell and her works. I especially wish to thank my family, who let me ignore many of life's "trifles" in order to find time to assemble this casebook.

Donna Winchell
Contributing Editor

Contents

Introduction

Trifles: Making It New

Susan Glaspell's first solo one-act play—a year earlier she had co-authored one with her husband George Gram "Jig" Cook—looked back to the events of December 2, 1900, in Indianola, Iowa, when a sixty-year-old farmer, John Hossack, was allegedly murdered by his wife of thirty-three years, Margaret, with two blows to the head with an ax. A news reporter for the *Des Moines Daily News* at the time, Glaspell noted in her coverage of the trial that like other trials, particularly those of a sensational nature, this one was well attended by women as well as men. Women could participate only as observers, though, since it would be a number of years before women in Iowa would be allowed to serve as jurors. Women's right to vote was still twenty years away.

Although Mrs. Hossack was convicted of the crime in her first trial (a later trial freed her), Glaspell chose to leave the legal outcome of the case unresolved when she adapted the story for the stage. The play concludes, however, with the clear implication that the men responsible for trying the case will fail to establish motive, while the women, in their identification with Mrs. Wright, the fictional equivalent of Mrs. Hossack, have determined the outcome of a trial in which they were supposed to participate only as bystanders. By de-emphasizing the legal decision, Glaspell places emphasis on the moral decisions made by women sensitive to Minnie Wright's plight and on the impact that societal pressures have on those moral decisions.

As Glaspell invites her audience into the disorderly kitchen of Minnie Wright's home in *Trifles*, she asks them to see with the play's characters that something has gone dreadfully wrong. It is not only that something has gone wrong with Minnie Wright. True, her rebellion against a life that gradually became unbearable took an unexpected and uncharacteristically violent form. There is something larger wrong, however, with a society that rewards domesticity above personal fulfillment. Mrs. Hale and Mrs. Peters choose a subtler means of rebelling against society's assumptions about gender. Theirs is a quiet rebellion, but it is typical of the sorts of rebellion that attracted Glaspell personally and professionally. Critical to an understanding of *Trifles* is an understanding of how women's roles were perceived in 1900 and continued to be viewed fifteen years later when the story of Margaret Hossack came to life on the stage.

THE NEW WOMAN EMERGES

Historians tend to view the years 1870–1920 as the era of the New Woman. The self-reliant "New Woman" was in direct conflict, however, with the concept of the submissive "True Woman" that was a particularly strong societal force in the last decade of the nineteenth century. Women of Glaspell's generation were caught in the middle.

Glaspell herself was torn between her feeling of obligation to conform to the roles expected of a woman in the opening decades of the twentieth century and her desire to let herself be guided by her own sense of morality. She never completely resolved that dilemma while her husband was alive except to the extent that she resolved it in her plays.

The True Woman was supposed to be moral, but early on Glaspell drew criticism from the townspeople in conservative Davenport when, as a young woman, she fell in love with and actively pursued Cook while he was still married to his second wife. Cook eventually left his wife and two children for Glaspell, who had by that point ceased being a lady by her society's standards. She joined a number of her friends in the practice, unconventional for that time, of keeping her maiden name after marriage.

Glaspell and Cook both wrote about the open nature of their marriage, and he was certainly not faithful to their marriage vows. Glaspell's adoration of her husband, however, is clear, particularly in her memoir of him, *The Road to the Temple*, which was published three years after his death. The True Woman is supposed to be subservient, and, once married to Cook, Glaspell took on a subservient role more in keeping with the True Woman than with the New Woman. She willingly, if perhaps with some silent regrets, gave up her fiction writing for a number of years to support him in his dream of founding a uniquely American theater. In that sense, she sacrificed her own desires to conform to her husband's. Cook's daughter from his second marriage makes clear that this was typical of Glaspell. She writes of Glaspell, "She subordinated herself completely, always to the man of the moment, was *anything* but a feminist, and always sad when work of her own succeeded more than my father's—or after, Norman Matson's" (Makowsky 7). After Cook's death, Glaspell was unconventional enough to live with Matson without the benefit of a marriage license, but not enough to take him home with her to Davenport.

The True Woman was supposed to be pious, yet Veronica Makowsky tells us how a young Glaspell could be found "spending Tuesdays with Davenport ladies at their study group, The Tuesday Club, while on Sundays eschewing church in favor of the socialists and reformers of the Monist Club" (17–18). Glaspell was attracted to socialism, as other feminists have been, because of the equality that it promises women.

In her plays, Glaspell fought the stereotype of the True Woman by highlighting its limitations. It is easy for contemporary readers to forget how limited most women's options were at and near the turn of the century. America celebrates the pioneer spirit, but the life that a woman had to lead on the plains of the Midwest even after the twentieth century began could be overwhelmingly lonely. The cult of domesticity preached that keeping house and taking care of family were a high calling—and should be enough for any woman. In Minnie Wright, however, Glaspell presents a character who, through her actions, shows they are not. Although Margaret Hossack had nine children, her fictional counterpart has none, making her domestic situation incomplete by definition. The men in the play judge Minnie Wright on her failure to conform to the cult of domesticity. They see her disordered kitchen as evidence of that failure.

Left alone on the stage, the women start to realize how completely society has failed Minnie. At worst, she may be abused by her husband. At best, she is isolated on a remote farm and denied even the bit of company a telephone would have provided her. Her husband is so unpleasant that neighbors stop visiting. She eventually gives up her few social activities because she is embarrassed by her shabby clothes. Her "voice" is taken away from her when she gives up singing in the church and thus loses one more association with a supportive community. The final straw that triggers her murdering her husband comes when he kills the canary that is her only pleasant companion and whose death symbolizes Wright's silencing of his wife. Mrs. Hale, from a neighboring farm, knows that she must bear in part the guilt for Mrs. Wright's loneliness; her friendship and support could have made a difference. Mrs. Peters, the sheriff's wife, can well understand the isolation Mrs. Wright felt day after day on the farm with no children to care for. She knew the same desolation when her first child died at the age of two and she faced the stillness and emptiness of the Dakotas.

WHENCE REFORM?

If Glaspell could not always live up to her feminist leanings, she could at least write about them, and her works have become feminist classics.

Because they emphasize the necessity for nonconformity, they also place her in the American transcendentalist tradition most often linked with Ralph Waldo Emerson, the nineteenth-century author and lecturer, perhaps best known for his essay "Self-Reliance." Makowsky has pointed out that Glaspell would have had Emerson include women when he wrote, "Whoso would be a man, must be a nonconformist," but that she also understood the justice of his comment that "for nonconformity the world whips you with its displeasure." If there is hope for change in society, it must come from within the individual, and reform will come at the hands of reformed individuals. Makowsky explains, "Since spirit dwells within each individual, his or her duty is to that spirit, not to social conventions" (7–8). She continues, "Glaspell wanted the benefits of society; companionship, a sense of structure, a sense of the past; she wanted these positive aspects to continue into the better future to which the Monist Club[1] was pointing. A smooth, gently upswinging curve was her ideal, not the wrenching motion of a pendulum, and in these early years, she and her fellow idealists believed it was possible, even for women" (18). In her later years, she put less faith in happy endings.

Glaspell did live to see women gain the right to serve on juries and, in 1920, to vote. She stressed the importance of women's right to be judged not just by men but also by women, their true peers, when she changed the title of *Trifles* to "A Jury of Her Peers" in transforming the play into a short story. When she died in 1948, however, America was still far from guaranteeing those who were accused of crimes the right to a trial by a jury of their peers, since the Civil Rights movement was just beginning.

In spite of its dates of initial production and publication, nothing in the play directly links it to the fact that America was on the brink of war. The timing of its publication, however, may explain why it was allowed to go out of print along with her other works after her death in 1948, despite the Pulitzer Prize that Glaspell was awarded in 1930 for her play *Alison's House*. Linda Ben-Zvi has pointed out that the 1950s in America, when Rosie the Riveter was taking off her overalls to put back on an apron, were not a time when Glaspell's works could be appreciated: "It takes a period not threatened by suggestions of cultural change to apprise such writing, such ideas, and such women adequately" (2). That time came in the United States in the 1970s with the birth of feminist theory, and *Trifles* and "A Jury of Her Peers" were among the first works to earn a last-

---

[1] Monist Club: a group of free-thinkers in Davenport who believed in the essential unity of mind and matter.

ing place in the anthologies of women's literature—and in anthologies of American literature in general (Ben-Zvi 2).

BRINGING GREEK THEATER TO MASSACHUSETTS

Greenwich Village, a section of New York City that teemed with artists and was famous for its bohemian way of life, provided a fitting home for Glaspell and Cook after their marriage in 1913. There the couple made lasting friends and got in on the beginning of the "little theater" movement, which put innovative native drama that could be staged at little expense up against the commercialism of Broadway. The flurry of excitement there made Cook determined to create his own little theater, and he chose to do so in Provincetown, Massachusetts, on Cape Cod, where he and his wife had honeymooned and where they spent their summers.

Cook was a flamboyant dreamer with the remarkable power to inspire others to make his dreams a reality. The vision behind the Provincetown Players was to bring something of the spirit of ancient Greek theater to America. Where his wife dreamed on a smaller scale of revolutionizing America, starting within the hearts and souls of reformed individuals, Cook envisioned change on a slightly larger scale, led by artists coordinating their efforts in bringing about change: "Suppose the nascence depends not on blind evolutionary forces, involving the whole nation, but on whether or not the hundred artists who have in them potential power arrange or do not arrange to place themselves in vital stimulating relationship with each other, in order to bring out, co-ordinate and direct their power" (qtd. in Waterman 47). He turned for his model to ancient Greece:

> He felt that Greece had proved that man could build a unified culture where the workaday and artistic worlds were united; where the businessmen, artisans, and politicians supported and created an artistic climate; where the cultural heritage, both real and legendary, formed the basis for art; and Cook recognized that this unity of life and art was most evident in the Greek theater. (Waterman 47–48)

The American equivalent was the noble pioneering spirit, which he felt had unfortunately given place to commercialism (Waterman 48).

The creation of the Provincetown Players was certainly a pioneering adventure in the staging of drama. The Players' home was literally a converted fishhouse across the road from Cook and Glaspell's summer home. It was particularly convenient for plays about the sea because the back wall consisted of sliding doors that looked out across the harbor, and the sound of the waves hitting the pilings provided natural sound effects. It may have been rough, but it was an important step in the history of American drama: It showcased American drama, instead of importing European drama, and allowed experimentation. The playwright directed his or her own plays and often acted in them. Seats may have been uncomfortable, but they were cheap.

It wasn't long before Cook moved his theater to New York under the fitting name of the Playwrights' Theater. Before long, however, the experimental theater as he had envisioned it died under its own weight. When plays were so successful at the Playwrights' Theater that they moved within two weeks to Broadway, he shut his theater down (Waterman 49). During the theater's brief stay in Provincetown, however, two playwrights clearly stood above the rest as most talented: Eugene O'Neill and Susan Glaspell.

O'Neill's name certainly comes closer to being a household name today than Susan Glaspell's. Although there are conflicting accounts as to how O'Neill's relationship with the Provincetown Players began, there is no question that the relationship proved to be a fortuitous one, since he needed a place to produce his plays at just the time when the Players needed good plays to produce. There is a consensus that O'Neill would have gone on to make a name for himself even if the Provincetown Players had never existed, but producing his plays on Cape Cod provided him an important step toward producing them on Broadway.

The impact that the Provincetown Players had on the relationship between Broadway and the little theaters in general is part of why Susan Glaspell and her husband are remembered as significant figures in the history of American drama. The little theaters had been established in response to the business ethics of Broadway. Proven formulas were what would "sell" on Broadway, so that was what was offered for public consumption. Experimentation was too risky when the bottom line was uppermost in the minds of the decision makers. What Cook and Glaspell helped to prove with such plays as *Trifles* was that there was a place in American drama for plays of ideas. American drama was moving toward realism, and the Provincetown Players were leading the way.

Glaspell's plays are not formulaic. *Trifles* is less experimental than some of her later plays, but Ben-Zvi has pointed out that even in *Trifles* there is nothing linear: "Nothing in a Glaspell play is linear. Plots do not have clearly defined beginnings, middles, and ends; they self-consciously move out from some familiar pattern, calling attention as they go to the fact that the expected convention will be violated, the anticipated order will be sundered" (qtd. in Makowsky 60). Little action takes place in *Trifles*. By the end of the play the two women who have come to Minnie's kitchen have moved close enough together in their thinking that they reveal their decision to conceal evidence through hurried action rather than through words.

Arthur Waterman succinctly sums up Glaspell's influence:

Miss Glaspell's work at the Provincetown was a major reason for the appearance of new realistic plays on Broadway about 1920 . . . the Provincetown created a climate where original plays by American playwrights were acceptable to the Broadway producers and to the theater public. The sudden outbreak of new realistic plays in the 1920s was no accident. Miss Glaspell's plays of ideas, which experimented with various techniques in order to create an intellectual drama, and the Playwright's Theatre's conspicuous achievement were important aspects of the rise of modern American drama. (90)

WORKS CITED

Ben-Zvi, Linda. "Introduction." Susan Glaspell: Essays on Her Theater and Fiction. U of Michigan P, 1995.

Bigsby, C. W. E. "Introduction." Susan Glaspell: Plays. Cambridge: Cambridge UP, 1987. 1–31.

Gould, Jean. "Susan Glaspell and the Provincetown Players." In Modern American Playwrights. New York: Dodd. 1966. 26–49.

Makowsky, Veronica. Susan Glaspell's Century of American Women: A Critical Interpretation of Her Work. Oxford UP, 1993.

Ozieblo, Barbara. Susan Glaspell: A Critical Biography. Chapel Hill: U of North Carolina P, 2000.

Waterman, Arthur E. Susan Glaspell. New York: Twayne, 1966.

Literature

About the Author:
Susan Glaspell

The career of playwright and fiction writer **Susan Glaspell (1876–1948)** has in some ways paralleled that of her African-American contemporary Zora Neale Hurston. Although Glaspell's works received more recognition during her lifetime than did Hurston's, both women's works went out of print before being "resurrected" during the last decades of the twentieth century through the efforts of feminists who sought to rediscover the works of America's lost women writers. Hurston's flamboyant lifestyle sometimes attracted attention that should have gone to her work; after she died in relative obscurity in Florida, her fame was reestablished largely through the efforts of fellow novelist Alice Walker. Glaspell's bohemian lifestyle led her from staid Davenport, Iowa, where she was born, first to Chicago and then eventually to Greenwich Village. It was a desire to escape with her husband, George Cram "Jig" Cook, from the heat of New York summers that led Glaspell to take a temporary break from her fiction writing to immerse herself in the world of the theater.

Glaspell left Davenport to attend Drake University but returned in 1901 to work as a reporter for a local newspaper. Her duties included covering the legislature and the social scene. Soon they also included reporting on the Hossack murder case, about which she wrote numerous articles that showed an increasing sympathy for the woman accused of murdering her husband with two ax blows to the head, particularly after she heard Mrs. Hossack's testimony and visited the Hossack home. Memories of the murder scene that she visited in 1901 would return to her in 1915 when her husband encouraged her to take up playwriting.

By the time Glaspell married Cook in 1913, she was already a successful writer. She had published short stories in periodicals and in a collection entitled *Lifted Masks* (1912), as well as two novels, *The Glory of the Conquered* (1909) and *The Visioning* (1911). Cook had a flair for the dramatic, however, that led to his dream of founding a community theater in Provincetown, Massachusetts, where he and his wife spent their summers with other refugees from New York. Glaspell and Cook found Broadway theater disappointing and shared a desire to establish in Provincetown a theater that would showcase American plays and that would not be limited by financial concerns.

Since Glaspell did not feel bound by the need to make her plays profitable, she felt free to experiment with new forms. After the success of the first season of the Provincetown Players, Cook announced a play by Glaspell for the next bill. Although for the first season Glaspell and Cook had enjoyed co-authoring *Suppressed Desires*, which poked gentle fun at the recent popularity of the theories of Sigmund Freud, now Glaspell undertook writing a play on her own. As she sat in the deserted fish-house, she saw taking shape on the stage before her the kitchen of the Hossack home she had visited as a reporter. Writing at a time when women did not yet have the right to serve on juries, Glaspell chose to have two female characters serve as judge and jury for a woman accused of murdering her husband. She named the one-act play *Trifles* because the men in the play who seek a motivation for the murder see women's work as too "trifling" to be of any significance, too much of the world of women, while the women realize that the very "trifles" the men disparage reveal just the motivation they seek.

Trifles was first produced in 1915 and first published in 1920 in a collection that included Glaspell's other one-act plays and her first full-length drama, *Bernice*. By

The Provincetown Playhouse, New York City, 1963
(originally called the Playwright's Theater)

that time the Provincetown Players had moved to New York to become the Playwrights' Theater. Two more of Glaspell's plays, *Inheritors* (1921) and *Chains of Dew* (unpublished) were produced at the New York location, but by the time the latter was produced in 1922, Glaspell and Cook were on their way to Greece, where Cook died in 1924. Three years later, in 1927, Glaspell published her memoir of her husband, *The Road to the Temple*.

Glaspell never reestablished a close relationship to the Playwrights' Theater after her husband's death. She did, however, become lovers with Normal Matson and together, in 1928, they wrote a play called *The Comic Artist*. Her playwriting career peaked in 1930 when her play *Alison's House* was awarded the Pulitzer Prize in drama. By that time she had largely turned away from playwriting and back to fiction. She continued to write novels until she died of viral pneumonia in 1948.

Trifles

(1916)

CHARACTERS

GEORGE HENDERSON, *county attorney*
HENRY PETERS, *sheriff*
LEWIS HALE, *a neighboring farmer*
MRS. PETERS
MRS. HALE

SCENE

The kitchen in the now abandoned farmhouse of John Wright, a gloomy kitchen, and left without having been put in order—unwashed pans under the sink, a loaf of bread outside the breadbox, a dish towel on the table—other signs of incompleted work. At the rear the outer door opens and the Sheriff comes in followed by the County Attorney and Hale. The Sheriff and Hale are men in middle life, the County Attorney is a young man; all are much bundled up and go at once to the stove. They are followed by two women—the Sheriff's wife first; she is a slight wiry woman, a thin nervous face. Mrs. Hale is larger and would ordinarily be called more comfortable looking, but she is disturbed now and looks fearfully about as she enters. The women have come in slowly, and stand close together near the door.

COUNTY ATTORNEY: *(rubbing his hands)* This feels good. Come up to the fire, ladies.

MRS. PETERS: *(after taking a step forward)* I'm not—cold.

SHERIFF: *(unbuttoning his overcoat and stepping away from the stove as if to mark the beginning of official business)* Now, Mr. Hale, before we move things about, you explain to Mr. Henderson just what you saw when you came here yesterday morning.

COUNTY ATTORNEY: By the way, has anything been moved? Are things just as you left them yesterday?

SHERIFF: *(looking about)* It's just the same. When it dropped below zero last night I thought I'd better send Frank out this morning to make a

5

fire for us—no use getting pneumonia with a big case on, but I told
him not to touch anything except the stove—and you know Frank.

COUNTY ATTORNEY: Somebody should have been left here yesterday.

SHERIFF: Oh—yesterday. When I had to send Frank to Morris Center
for that man who went crazy—I want you to know I had my hands
full yesterday. I knew you could get back from Omaha by today and
as long as I went over everything here myself—

COUNTY ATTORNEY: Well, Mr. Hale, tell just what happened when you
came here yesterday morning.

HALE: Harry and I had started to town with a load of potatoes. We came
along the road from my place and as I got here I said, "I'm going to
see if I can't get John Wright to go in with me on a party telephone."
I spoke to Wright about it once before and he put me off, saying folks
talked too much anyway, and all he asked was peace and quiet—
I guess you know about how much he talked himself; but I thought
maybe if I went to the house and talked about it before his wife,
though I said to Harry that I didn't know as what his wife wanted
made much difference to John—

COUNTY ATTORNEY: Let's talk about that later, Mr. Hale. I do want to talk   10
about that, but tell now just what happened when you got to the
house.

HALE: I didn't hear or see anything; I knocked at the door, and still it
was all quiet inside. I knew they must be up, it was past eight
o'clock. So I knocked again, and I thought I heard somebody say,
"Come in." I wasn't sure, I'm not sure yet, but I opened the door—
this door (*indicating the door by which the two woman are still
standing*) and there in that rocker—(*pointing to it*) sat Mrs. Wright.

They all look at the rocker.

COUNTY ATTORNEY: What—was she doing?

HALE: She was rockin' back and forth. She had her apron in her hand
and was kind of—pleating it.

COUNTY ATTORNEY: And how did she—look?

HALE: Well, she looked queer.   15

COUNTY ATTORNEY: How do you mean—queer?

HALE: Well, as if she didn't know what she was going to do next. And
kind of done up.

COUNTY ATTORNEY: How did she seem to feel about your coming?

HALE: Why I don't think she minded—one way or other. She didn't pay
much attention. I said, "How do, Mrs. Wright, it's cold, ain't it?" And

she said, "Is it?"—and went on kind of pleating at her apron. Well, I was surprised; she didn't ask me to come up to the stove, or to set down, but just sat there, not even looking at me, so I said, "I want to see John." And then she—laughed. I guess you would call it a laugh. I thought of Harry and the team outside, so I said a little sharp: "Can't I see John?" "No," she says, kind o' dull like. "Ain't he home?" says I. "Yes," says she, "he's home." "Then why can't I see him?" I asked her, out of patience. " 'Cause he's dead," says she. *"Dead?"* says I. She just nodded her head, not getting a bit excited, but rockin' back and forth. "Why—where is he?" says I, not knowing what to say. She just pointed upstairs—like that. *(Himself pointing to the room above.)* I got up, with the idea of going up there. I walked from there to here— then I says, "Why, what did he die of?" "He died of a rope around his neck," says she, and just went on pleatin' at her apron. Well, I went out and called Harry. I thought I might—need help. We went upstairs and there he was lyin'—

COUNTY ATTORNEY: I think I'd rather have you go into that upstairs, where you can point it all out. Just go on now with the rest of the story.   20

HALE: Well, my first thought was to get that rope off. It looked . . . *(stops, his face twitched)* . . . but Harry, he went up to him, and he said, "No, he's dead all right, and we'd better not touch anything." So we went back down stairs. She was still sitting that same way. "Has anybody been notified?" I asked. "No," says she, unconcerned. "Who did this, Mrs. Wright?" said Harry. He said it businesslike—and she stopped pleatin' of her apron. "I don't know," she says. "You don't *know?*" says Harry. "No," says she. "Weren't you sleepin' in the bed with him?" says Harry. "Yes," says she, "but I was on the inside." "Somebody slipped a rope round his neck and strangled him and you didn't wake up?" says Harry. "I didn't wake up," she said after him. We must 'a looked as if we didn't see how that could be, for after a minute she said, "I sleep sound." Harry was going to ask her more questions but I said maybe we ought to let her tell her story first to the coroner, or the sheriff, so Harry went fast as he could to Rivers' place, where there's a telephone.

COUNTY ATTORNEY: And what did Mrs. Wright do when she knew that you had gone for the coroner?

HALE: She moved from that chair to this one over here *(pointing to a small chair in the corner)* and just sat there with her hands held together and looking down. I got a feeling that I ought to make some conversation, so I said I had come in to see if John wanted to put in a telephone, and at that she started to laugh, and then she stopped and looked at me—scared. *(The County Attorney, who has had his notebook out, makes a note.)* I dunno, maybe it wasn't scared. I wouldn't like to say it was. Soon Harry got back, and then Dr. Lloyd came, and you, Mr. Peters, and so I guess that's all I know that you don't.

COUNTY ATTORNEY: *(looking around)* I guess we'll go upstairs first—and then out to the barn and around there. *(To the Sheriff.)* You're convinced that there was nothing important here—nothing that would point to any motive.

SHERIFF: Nothing here but kitchen things. 25

The County Attorney, after again looking around the kitchen, opens the door of a cupboard closet. He gets up on a chair and looks on a shelf. Pulls his hand away, sticky.

COUNTY ATTORNEY: Here's a nice mess.

The women draw nearer.

MRS. PETERS: *(to the other woman)* Oh, her fruit; it did freeze. *(To the County Attorney.)* She worried about that when it turned so cold. She said the fire'd go out and her jars would break.

SHERIFF: Well, can you beat the woman! Held for murder and worryin' about her preserves.

COUNTY ATTORNEY: I guess before we're through she may have something more serious than preserves to worry about.

HALE: Well, women are used to worrying over trifles. 30

The two women move a little closer together.

COUNTY ATTORNEY: *(with the gallantry of a young politician)* And yet, for all their worries, what would we do without the ladies? *(The women do not unbend. He goes to the sink, takes a dipperful of water from the pail and pouring it into a basin, washes his hands. Starts to wipe them on the roller towel, turns it for a cleaner place.)* Dirty towels! *(Kicks his foot against the pans under the sink.)* Not much of a housekeeper, would you say, ladies?

MRS. HALE: *(stiffly)* There's a great deal of work to be done on a farm.

COUNTY ATTORNEY: To be sure. And yet *(with a little bow to her)* I know there are some Dickson county farmhouses which do not have such roller towels.

He gives it a pull to expose its full length again.

MRS. HALE: Those towels get dirty awful quick. Men's hands aren't always as clean as they might be.

COUNTY ATTORNEY: Ah, loyal to your sex, I see. But you and Mrs. Wright 35 were neighbors. I suppose you were friends, too.

MRS. HALE: *(shaking her head)* I've not seen much of her of late years. I've not been in this house—it's more than a year.

COUNTY ATTORNEY: And why was that? You didn't like her?

MRS. HALE: I liked her well enough. Farmer's wives have their hands full, Mr. Henderson. And then—

County Attorney: Yes—?

MRS. HALE: *(looking about)* It never seemed a very cheerful place. 40

COUNTY ATTORNEY: No—it's not cheerful. I shouldn't say she had the homemaking instinct.

MRS. HALE: Well, I don't know as Wright had, either.

COUNTY ATTORNEY: You mean that they didn't get on very well?

MRS. HALE: No, I don't mean anything. But I don't think a place'd be any cheerfuller for John Wright's being in it.

COUNTY ATTORNEY: I'd like to talk more of that a little later. I want to get 45 the lay of things upstairs now.

He goes to the left, where three steps lead to a stair door.

SHERIFF: I suppose anything Mrs. Peters does'll be all right. She was to take in some clothes for her, you know, and a few little things. We left in such a hurry yesterday.

COUNTY ATTORNEY: Yes, but I would like to see what you take, Mrs. Peters, and keep an eye out for anything that might be of use to us.

MRS. PETERS: Yes, Mr. Henderson.

The women listen to the men's steps on the stairs, then look about the kitchen.

MRS. HALE: I'd hate to have men coming into my kitchen, snooping around and criticizing.

She arranges the pans under the sink which the County Attorney had shoved out of place.

MRS. PETERS: Of course it's no more than their duty. 50

MRS. HALE: Duty's all right, but I guess that deputy sheriff that came out to make the fire might have got a little of this on. *(Gives the roller towel a pull.)* Wish I'd thought of that a little sooner. Seems

mean to talk about her for not having things slicked up when she
had to come away in such a hurry.

MRS. PETERS: *(who has gone to a small table in the left rear of the room,
and lifted one end of a towel that covers a pan)* She had bread set.

Stands still.

MRS. HALE: *(eyes fixed on a loaf of bread beside the breadbox, which is on
a low shelf at the other side of the room. Moves slowly toward it.)* She
was going to put this in there. *(Picks up loaf, then abruptly drops it.
In a manner of returning to familiar things.)* It's a shame about her
fruit. I wonder if it's all gone. *(Gets up on the chair and looks.)* I think
there's some here that's all right, Mrs. Peters. Yes—here; *(holding it
toward the window)* this is cherries, too. *(Looking again.)* I declare I
believe that's the only one. *(Gets down, bottle in her hand. Goes to the
sink and wipes it off on the outside.)* She'll feel awful bad after all her
hard work in the hot weather. I remember the afternoon I put up my
cherries last summer.

*She puts the bottle on the big kitchen table, center of the room. With
a sigh, is about to sit down in the rocking-chair. Before she is seated
realized what chair it is; with a slow look at it, steps back. The chair
which she has touched rocks back and forth.*

MRS. PETERS: Well, I must get those things from the front room closet.
*(She goes to the door at the right, but after looking into the other
room, steps back.)* You coming with me, Mrs. Hale? You could help me
carry them.

*They go in the other room; reappear, Mrs. Peters carrying a dress and
skirt, Mrs. Hale following with a pair of shoes.*

MRS. PETERS: My, it's cold in there.   55

She puts the clothes on the big table, and hurries to the stove.

MRS. HALE: *(examining her skirt)* Wright was close. I think maybe that's
why she kept so much to herself. She didn't even belong to the Ladies
Aid. I suppose she felt she couldn't do her part, and then you don't
enjoy things when you feel shabby. She used to wear pretty clothes
and be lively, when she was Minnie Foster, one of the town girls
singing in the choir. But that—oh, that was thirty years ago. This all
you was to take in?

MRS. PETERS: She said she wanted an apron. Funny thing to want, for there isn't much to get you dirty in jail, goodness knows. But I suppose just to make her feel more natural. She said they was in the top drawer in this cupboard. Yes, here. And then her little shawl that always hung behind the door. *(Opens stair door and looks.)* Yes, here it is.

Quickly shuts door leading upstairs.

MRS. HALE: *(abruptly moving toward her)* Mrs. Peters?

MRS. PETERS: Yes, Mrs. Hale?

MRS. HALE: Do you think she did it?　　　　　　　　　　　　　　　　60

MRS. PETERS: *(in a frightened voice)* Oh, I don't know.

MRS. HALE: Well, I don't think she did. Asking for an apron and her little shawl. Worrying about her fruit.

MRS. PETERS: *(starts to speak, glances up, where footsteps are heard in the room above. In a low voice.)* Mr. Peters says it looks bad for her. Mr. Henderson is awful sarcastic in a speech and he'll make fun of her sayin' she didn't wake up.

MRS. HALE: Well, I guess John Wright didn't wake up when they was slipping that rope under his neck.

MRS. PETERS: No, it's strange. It must have been down awful crafty and　　65
still. They say it was such a—funny way to kill a man, rigging it all up like that.

MRS. HALE: That's just what Mr. Hale said. There was a gun in the house. He says that's what he can't understand.

MRS. PETERS: Mr. Henderson said coming out that what was needed for the case was a motive; something to show anger, or—sudden feeling.

MRS. HALE: *(who is standing by the table)* Well, I don't see any signs of anger around here. *(She puts her hand on the dish towel which lies on the table, stands looking down at table, one half of which is clean, the other half messy.)* It's wiped to here. *(Makes a move as if to finish work, then turns and looks at loaf of bread outside the breadbox. Drops towel. In that voice of coming back to familiar things.)* Wonder how they are finding things upstairs. I hope she had it a little more red-up[1] up there. You know, it seems kind of sneaking. Locking her up in town and then coming out here and trying to get her own house to turn against her!

---

[1] Spruced up. (slang)

MRS. PETERS: But Mrs. Hale, the law is the law.

MRS. HALE: I s'pose 'tis. *(Unbuttoning her coat.)* Better loosen up your   70
things, Mrs. Peters. You won't feel them when you go out.

Mrs. Peters takes off her fur tippet, goes to hang it on the hook at back of room, stands looking at the under part of the small corner table.

MRS. PETERS: She was piecing a quilt.

She brings the large sewing basket and they look at the bright pieces.

MRS. HALE: It's log cabin pattern. Pretty, isn't it? I wonder if she was goin' to quilt it or just knot it?

Footsteps have been heard coming down the stairs. The Sheriff enters followed by Hale and the County Attorney.

SHERIFF: They wonder if she was going to quilt it or just knot it!

The men laugh; the women look abashed.

COUNTY ATTORNEY: *(rubbing his hands over the stove)* Frank's fire didn't do much up there, did it? Well, let's go out to the barn and get that cleared up.

The men go outside.

MRS. HALE: *(resentfully)* I don't know as there's anything so strange, our   75
takin' up time with little things while we're waiting for them to get the evidence. *(She sits down at the big table smoothing out a block with decision.)* I don't see as it's anything to laugh about.

MRS. PETERS: *(apologetically)* Of course they've got awful important things on their minds.

Pulls up a chair and joins Mrs. Hale at the table.

MRS. HALE: *(examining another block)* Mrs. Peters, look at this one. Here, this is the one she was working on, and look at the sewing! All the rest of it has been so nice and even. And look at this! It's all over the place! Why, it looks as if she didn't know what she was about!

After she has said this they look at each other, then start to glance back at the door. After an instant Mrs. Hale has pulled at a knot and ripped the sewing.

MRS. PETERS: Oh, what are you doing, Mrs. Hale?

MRS. HALE: *(mildly)* Just pulling out a stitch or two that's not sewed very good. *(Threading a needle.)* Bad sewing always made me fidgety.

MRS. PETERS: *(nervously)* I don't think we ought to touch things.   80

MRS. HALE: I'll just finish up this end. *(Suddenly stopping and leaning forward.)* Mrs. Peters?

MRS. PETERS: Yes, Mrs. Hale?

MRS. HALE: What do you suppose she was so nervous about?

MRS. PETERS: Oh—I don't know. I don't know as she was nervous. I sometimes sew awful queer when I'm just tired. *(Mrs. Hale starts to say something, looks at Mrs. Peters, then goes on sewing.)* Well, I must get these things wrapped up. They may be through sooner than we think. *(Putting apron and other things together.)* I wonder where I can find a piece of paper, and string.

MRS. HALE: In that cupboard, maybe.   85

MRS. PETERS: *(looking in cupboard)* Why, here's a birdcage. *(Holds it up.)* Did she have a bird, Mrs. Hale?

MRS. HALE: Why, I don't know whether she did or not—I've not been here for so long. There was a man around last year selling canaries cheap, but I don't know as she took one; maybe she did. She used to sing real pretty herself.

MRS. PETERS: *(glancing around)* Seems funny to think of a bird here. But she must have had one, or why would she have a cage? I wonder what happened to it.

MRS. HALE: I s'pose maybe the cat got it.

MRS. PETERS: No, she didn't have a cat. She's got that feeling some   90 people have about cats—being afraid of them. My cat got in her room and she was real upset and asked me to take it out.

MRS. HALE: My sister Bessie was like that. Queer, ain't it?

MRS. PETERS: *(examining the cage)* Why, look at this door. It's broke. One hinge is pulled apart.

MRS. HALE: *(looking too)* Looks as if someone must have been rough with it.

MRS. PETERS: Why, yes.

She brings the cage forward and puts it on the table.

MRS. HALE: I wish if they're going to find any evidence they'd be about   95 it. I don't like this place.

MRS. PETERS: But I'm awful glad you came with me, Mrs. Hale. It would be lonesome for me sitting here alone.

MRS. HALE: It would, wouldn't it? *(Dropping her sewing.)* But I tell you what I do wish, Mrs. Peters. I wish I had come over sometimes when *she* was here. I—*(looking around the room)*—wish I had.

MRS. PETERS: But of course you were awful busy, Mrs. Hale—your house and your children.

MRS. HALE: I could've come. I stayed away because it weren't cheerful—and that's why I ought to have come. I—I've never liked this place. Maybe because it's down in a hollow and you don't see the road. I dunno what it is but it's a lonesome place and always was. I wish I had come over to see Minnie Foster sometimes. I can see now—

Shakes her head.

MRS. PETERS: Well, you mustn't reproach yourself, Mrs. Hale. Somehow   100
we just don't see how it is with other folks until—something comes up.

MRS. HALE: Not having children makes less work—but it makes a quiet house, and Wright out to work all day, and no company when he did come in. Did you know John Wright, Mrs. Peters?

MRS. PETERS: Not to know him; I've seen him in town. They say he was a good man.

MRS. HALE: Yes—good; he didn't drink, and kept his word as well as most, I guess, and paid his debts. But he was a hard man, Mrs. Peters. Just to pass the time of day with him—*(Shivers.)* Like a raw wind that gets to the bone. *(Pauses, her eye falling on the cage.)* I should think she would 'a wanted a bird. But what do you suppose went with it?

MRS. PETERS: I don't know, unless it got sick and died.

She reaches over and swings the broken door, swings it again. Both women watch it.

MRS. HALE: You weren't raised round here, were you? *(Mrs. Peters*   105
shakes her head.) You didn't know—her?

MRS. PETERS: Not till they brought her yesterday.

MRS. HALE: She—come to think of it, she was kind of like a bird herself—real sweet and pretty, but kind of timid and—fluttery. How—she—did—change. *(Silence; then as if struck by a happy thought and relieved to get back to everyday things.)* Tell you what, Mrs. Peters, why don't you take the quilt with you? It might take up her mind.

MRS. PETERS: Why, I think that's a real nice idea, Mrs. Hale. There couldn't possibly be any objection to it, could there? Now, just what would I take? I wonder if her patches are in here—and her things.

They look in the sewing basket.

MRS. HALE: Here's some red. I expect this has got sewing things in it. *(Brings out a fancy box.)* What a pretty box. Looks like something somebody would give you. Maybe her scissors are in here. *(Opens box. Suddenly puts her hand to her nose.)* Why—*(Mrs. Peters bends nearer, then turns her face away.)* There's something wrapped up in this piece of silk.

MRS. PETERS: Why, this isn't her scissors. 110

MRS. HALE: *(lifting the silk)* Oh, Mrs. Peters—it's—

Mrs. Peters bends closer.

MRS. PETERS: It's the bird.

MRS. HALE: *(jumping up)* But, Mrs. Peters—look at it! Look at its neck! It's all—other side *to.*

Their eyes meet. A look of growing comprehension, of horror. Steps are heard outside. Mrs. Hale slips box under quilt pieces, and sinks into her chair. Enter Sheriff and County Attorney. Mrs. Peters rises.

COUNTY ATTORNEY: *(as one turning from serious things to little pleas-* 115 *antries)* Well, ladies, have you decided whether she was going to quilt it or knot it?

MRS. PETERS: We think she was going to—knot it.

COUNTY ATTORNEY: Well, that's interesting, I'm sure. *(Seeing the bird-cage.)* Has the bird flown?

MRS. HALE: *(putting more quilt pieces over the box)* We think the—cat got it.

COUNTY ATTORNEY: *(preoccupied)* Is there a cat?

Mrs. Hale glances in a quick covert way at Mrs. Peters.

MRS. PETERS: Well, not *now.* They're superstitious, you know. They leave. 120

COUNTY ATTORNEY: *(to Sheriff Peters, continuing an interrupted conversa-tion)* No sign at all of anyone having come from the outside. Their own rope. Now let's go up again and go over it piece by piece. *(They start upstairs.)* It would have to have been someone who knew just the—

Mrs. Peters sits down. The two women sit there not looking at one another, but as if peering into something and at the same time holding back. When they talk now it is in the manner of feeling their way over strange ground, as if afraid of what they are saying, but as if they can not help saying it.

MRS. HALE: She liked the bird. She was going to bury it in that pretty
box.

MRS. PETERS: *(in a whisper)* When I was a girl—my kitten—there was a
boy took a hatchet, and before my eyes—and before I could get
there—*(Covers her face an instant.)* If they hadn't held me back I
would have—*(catches herself, looks upstairs where steps are heard,
falters weakly)*—hurt him.

MRS. HALE: *(with a slow look around her)* I wonder how it would seem
never to have had any children around. *(Pause.)* No, Wright wouldn't
like the bird—a thing that sang. She used to sing. He killed that, too.

MRS. PETERS: *(moving uneasily)* We don't know who killed the bird.   125

MRS. HALE: I knew John Wright.

MRS. PETERS: It was an awful thing was done in this house that night,
Mrs. Hale. Killing a man while he slept, slipping a rope around his
neck that choked the life out of him.

MRS. HALE: His neck. Choked the life out of him.

Her hand goes out and rests on the birdcage.

MRS. PETERS: *(with rising voice)* We don't know who killed him. We don't
know.

MRS. HALE: *(her own feeling not interrupted)* If there'd been years and   130
years of nothing, then a bird to sing to you, it would be awful—still,
after the bird was still.

MRS. PETERS: *(something within her speaking)* I know what stillness is.
When we homesteaded in Dakota, and my first baby died—after he
was two years old, and me with no other then—

MRS. HALE: *(moving)* How soon do you suppose they'll be through, looking for the evidence?

MRS. PETERS: I know what stillness is. *(Pulling herself back.)* The law
has got to punish crime, Mrs. Hale.

MRS. HALE: *(not as if answering that)* I wish you'd seen Minnie Foster
when she wore a white dress with blue ribbons and stood up there in
the choir and sang. *(A look around the room.)* Oh, I *wish* I'd come
over here once in a while! That was a crime! That was a crime! Who's
going to punish that?

MRS. PETERS: *(looking upstairs)* We mustn't—take on.   135

MRS. HALE: I might have known she needed help! I know how things
can be—for women. I tell you, it's queer, Mrs. Peters. We live close
together and we live far apart. We all go through the same things—

it's all just a different kind of the same thing. *(Brushes her eyes; noticing the bottle of fruit, reaches out for it.)* If I was you I wouldn't tell her her fruit was gone. Tell her it *ain't*. Tell her it's all right. Take this in to prove it to her. She—she may never know whether it was broke or not.

MRS. PETERS: *(takes the bottle, looks about for something to wrap it in; takes petticoat from the clothes brought from the other room, very nervously begins winding this around the bottle. In a false voice)* My, its a good thing the men couldn't hear us. Wouldn't they just laugh! getting all stirred up over a little thing like this—a dead canary. As if that could have anything to do with—with—wouldn't they *laugh!*

The men are heard coming down stairs.

MRS. HALE: *(under her breath)* Maybe they would—maybe they wouldn't.

COUNTY ATTORNEY: No, Peters, it's all perfectly clear except a reason for doing it. But you know juries when it comes to women. If there was some definite thing. Something to show—something to make a story about—a thing that would connect up with this strange way of doing it—

The women's eyes meet for an instant. Enter Hale from outer door.

HALE: Well, I've got the team around. Pretty cold out there.   140

COUNTY ATTORNEY: I'm going to stay here a while by myself. *(To the Sheriff.)* You can send Frank out for me, can't you? I want to go over everything. I'm not satisfied that we can't do better.

SHERIFF: Do you want to see what Mrs. Peters is going to take in?

The County Attorney goes to the table, picks up the apron, laughs.

COUNTY ATTORNEY: Oh, I guess they're not very dangerous things the ladies have picked out. *(Moves a few things about, disturbing the quilt pieces which cover the box. Steps back.)* No, Mrs. Peters doesn't need supervising. For that matter, a sheriff's wife is married to the law. Ever think of it that way, Mrs. Peters?

MRS. PETERS: Not—just that way.

SHERIFF: *(chuckling)* Married to the law. *(Moves toward the other room.)*   145
I just want you to come in here a minute, George. We ought to take a look at these windows.

COUNTY ATTORNEY: *(scoffingly)* Oh, windows!

SHERIFF: We'll be right out, Mr. Hale.

Hale goes outside. The Sheriff follows the County Attorney into the other room. Then Mrs. Hale rises, hands tight together, looking intensely at Mrs. Peters, whose eyes make a slow turn, finally meeting Mrs. Hale's. A moment Mrs. Hale holds her, then her own eyes point the way to where the box is concealed. Suddenly Mrs. Peters throws back quilt pieces and tries to put the box in the bag she is wearing. It is too big. She opens box, starts to take bird out, cannot touch it, goes to pieces, stands there help- less. Sound of a knob turning in the other room. Mrs. Hale snatches the box and puts it in the pocket of her big coat. Enter County Attorney and Sheriff.

COUNTY ATTORNEY: *(facetiously)* Well, Henry, at least we found out that she was not going to quilt it. She was going to—what is it you call it, ladies?

MRS. HALE: *(her hand against her pocket)* We call it—knot it, Mr. Henderson.

DISCUSSION QUESTIONS

1. Consider why Glaspell might have chosen the kitchen of the Wright home as the setting for *Trifles*. What details of that setting reflect plot and theme?

2. To what extent is the play a product of the time in which it was written and initially produced, and to what extent could the events of the play happen today?

3. The play is unusual for a murder mystery in that neither the victim nor the accused appears on stage. What effect does their absence have on the play? Is either Mr. Wright or Mrs. Wright the main character of the play? If not, who is?

4. In spite of the fact that we never see John Wright on stage, we tend to form an impression of the type of person he was. How do we obtain information about him? What impression does that information add up to regarding the type of person that he is?

5. Why does some conflict arise between the male and the female characters as they all look about the kitchen? Is that conflict ever resolved? Are we allowed insight into internal conflict going on within any of the characters?

6. Early in the play, when the County Attorney ridicules women for "worrying over trifles," Mrs. Hale and Mrs. Peters "move a little closer together" (18). In what ways do the two women move "closer together" in more than a physical sense before the play is over? How does the relationship between the two women—along with their relationship with the absent Minnie Foster—reveal the theme of the work?

7. What "trifles" do the women discover as they wait downstairs, and how do those "trifles" provide the motive for murder that the men, at the same time, are looking for upstairs?

8. Discuss the symbolism of the dead bird and its cage.

9. When *Trifles* was rewritten as a short story, Glaspell changed the title to "A Jury of Her Peers." Which title do you think better captures the theme of the play? Why?

10. There are numerous references in the play to quilting and knotting. Explain how these references suggest more than simply technical terms for two ways of making a quilt. What weight and meaning do all of those references give to Mrs. Hale's last words?

RESEARCH TOPICS

1. Analyze the differences between the facts of the Hossack case as described by Ben-Zvi and Glaspell's fictionalized account of the murder and the resulting trial. How did Glaspell reshape the facts to suit her artistic purposes, and to what effect?

2. View Sally Heckel's film version of "A Jury of Her Peers." How is this film different from the play? Do you feel the film presents a different perspective on the murder of John Wright and its aftermath from that presented in *Trifles*?

3. Read one of Glaspell's other plays, and discuss any similarities you see in her treatment of women and their role in society between that work and *Trifles*.

4. Research the role that Glaspell played in the founding of the Provincetown Players and explain why that role gave her the status of a major figure in the history of American drama.

5. When were women in Iowa first allowed to serve on juries? How does that bit of background information affect your reading of *Trifles*? How might it have affected how the play was viewed by Glaspell's contemporaries? Try to find some contemporary reviews of productions of Glaspell's work.

6. Use at least two of the secondary sources included here to explain why Glaspell's works were brought back into prominence in the second half of the twentieth century by feminist scholars.

7. Use sources included in this casebook and/or other sources to support your own reading of *Trifles* in terms of its portrayal of gender roles.

Secondary Sources

from "Murder, She Wrote": The Genesis of Susan Glaspell's *Trifles*

In the preface of her book *Women Who Kill* Ann Jones explains that her massive study of women murderers began with a quip. After working through a reading list that included *The Awakening*, *The House of Mirth*, and *The Bell Jar*, a student asked: "Isn't there anything a woman can do but kill herself?" Jones responded, "She can always kill somebody else" (xv).

Women killing somebody else, especially when that somebody is male, has fascinated criminologists, lawyers, psychologists, and writers. Fascinated and frightened them. Fear is the subtext of Jones's book: "The fears of men who, even as they shape society, are desperately afraid of women, and so have fashioned a world in which women come and go only in certain rooms; and about the fears of those women who, finding the rooms too narrow and the door still locked, lie in wait or set the place afire" (xvi). Or kill.

Women who kill evoke fear because they challenge societal constructs of femininity—passivity, restraint, and nurture—thus the rush to isolate and label the female offender, to cauterize her act. Her behavior *must* be aberrant, or crazed, if it is to be explicable. And explicable it must be; her crime cannot be seen as societally driven if the cultural stereotypes are to remain unchallenged.[1]

Theater loves a good murder story: violence, passion, and purpose. The stuff of tragedy is the stuff of the whodunit; *Oedipus* is, among other things, the Ur-detective story. Therefore, it is not surprising that contemporary dramatists should turn to murder—specifically, murder by women—as sources for plays. And following the thesis of Jones's book, it is also not surprising that the most powerful of the dramas—those that are more than exempla, docudramas, or hysterogenic flights—should be written by women who share with Jones an awareness that often the murderer, like the feminist, in her own way, "tests society's established boundaries" (13). . . .

The case at first glance seemed simple. Sometime after midnight on December 2, 1900, John Hossack, a well-to-do farmer, was struck twice on the head with an ax while he slept in bed. Margaret Hossack, his wife of thirty-three years, who was sleeping beside him, reported that a strange sound, "like two pieces of wood striking," wakened her; she jumped out of bed, went into the adjoining sitting room, saw a light shining on a wall, and heard the door to the front porch slowly closing. Only then did she hear her husband's groans. Assembling the five of her nine children who were still residing at home, she lit a lamp, reentered the bedroom, and discovered Hossack bleeding profusely, the walls and bedsheets spattered, his brain matter oozing from a five-inch gash, his head crushed. One of sons claimed that the mortally injured man was still able to speak. When he said to his father, "Well pa, you are badly hurt," Hossack replied, "No, I'm not hurt, but I'm not feeling well" (Dec. 4).

It was assumed that prowlers must have committed the crime, but, when a search of the farmhouse failed to reveal any missing items, a coroner's inquest was called. Its findings were inconclusive. However, after discovering the presumed murder weapon smeared with blood under the family corn crib, and listening to reports and innuendos from neighbors, who hinted at a history of marital and family trouble, the sheriff arrested Mrs. Hossack, "as a matter of precaution" (Dec. 5), while the funeral was still in progress, or, as Glaspell would more vividly report, "just as the sexton was throwing the last clods on the grave of her murdered husband" (Jan. 14) . . .

Employing the techniques of "Gonzo" journalism sixty years before Hunter Thompson, Glaspell filed twenty-six stories on the Hossack case, from the fifteen-line item on page 3, dated December 3, 1900, that summarily described the event of the murder, to the page 1, full-column story on April 11, 1901, that reported the jury's decision at the trial. Most are indistinguishable from her own unsigned "Newsgirl" features running in the paper at the time. They make ready use of hyperbole, invention, and supposition, all filtered through one of Glaspell's common devices in her column: a lively, often opinionated persona. Whether labeled "your correspondent," "a representative from the *News*," or "a member of the press," she is a constructed presence who invites the reader to share some privileged information, intriguing rumor, and running assessment of the case and of the guilt or innocence of the accused.

In her first extended coverage of the crime, under the headline "Coroner's Jury Returns Its Verdict This Morning—Mrs. Hossack Thought to Be Crazy," Glaspell announces the imminent arrest of the woman, a fact "secretly revealed to your correspondent." She also provides the first of many rumors that become increasingly more prominent in her coverage although never attributed to specific sources: "Friends of Mrs. Hossack are beginning to suggest that she is insane, and that she has been in this condition for a year and a half, under the constant surveillance of members of the family," and "the members of the Hossack family were not on pleasant relations with each other," information that comes as "a complete surprise, as Hossack was not supposed to have an enemy in the world." She concludes by citing the most damaging evidence used against the accused woman throughout her trial: Mrs. Hossack's claim that she lay asleep beside her husband and was not awakened while the murder was taking place (Dec. 5).

Glaspell continues to mix fact, rumor, and commentary with a superfluity of rousing language and imagery, opening her next report with the reminder that Mrs. Hossack has been arrested for the death of her husband, "on charge of having beaten out his brains with an axe"; that the accused woman has employed the legal services of Mr. Henderson and State Senator Berry; that when arrested she showed no emotion and absolutely declined to make any statement concerning her guilt or innocence; and that, while her family supported her, "the public sentiment is overwhelmingly against her." How she gleaned this information or arrived at these conclusions Glaspell does not say. She does, however, provide her first description of the accused woman: "Though past 50 years of age, she is tall and powerful and looks like she would be dangerous if aroused to a point of hatred." She again repeats the rumors of domestic tensions and quotes a neighbor named Haines, a witness at the inquest, who implied that Mrs. Hossack had years before asked him to get her husband "out of the way" (Dec. 6). . . .

In the months before the trial Glaspell filed only three small articles about the case, each one using the opportunity of a new piece of news to summarize the details of the murder, the grisly events becoming more grisly with the retelling. On March 23 she reports that new evidence has emerged "and that in all probability it would result in Mrs. Hossack's acquittal at an early date." She does not say what the evidence is, but she offers an important turn in the case. Mr. Haines, the primary source of information about trouble in the Hossack home and the party to whom, it is believed, Mrs. Hossack turned to get rid of her husband, "had gone insane brooding over the tragedy, and was yesterday sentenced to the insane asylum."

Although there had been talk of moving the venue of the trial because of the strong feelings against Margaret Hossack and the fear that an impartial jury could not be found (Jan. 14), the trial finally began in the Polk County Courthouse on April 1, 1901, and was held every day except Sundays for the next ten days. Glaspell had apparently been successful in stirring public interest because she reports that on the first day over twelve hundred people attended, far more than the tiny rural court could accommodate, and that on the day the jury returned its verdict more than two thousand were present. Noting the composition of the observers, she says: "The conspicuous feature so far is the large attendance of women in court. Over half of the spectators present today belong to the gentler sex. The bright array of Easter hats lent a novelty to the scene, giving it much the appearance of some social function" (Apr. 2).[2]

The seventy-eight witnesses, fifty-three for the prosecution and twenty-five for the defense, focused on seven specific questions during the trial: (1) Would it have been possible, as his son testified, for John Hossack, who had sustained two traumatic blows—one made with the ax head, the second with the blunt handle—to talk and call for his wife and children? (2) Were the blood found on the ax and the hairs later discovered nearby human, or were they, as claimed by the family, the residue of the turkey killed two days earlier for Thanksgiving? (3) How had the ax, which the youngest son said he placed inside the corn crib after killing the turkey, come to be found under it, in its usual place? (4) Had the ax and Mrs. Hossack's nightclothes been washed to remove incriminating stains of blood? (5) Was the dog, who always barked when strangers appeared, drugged on the night of the crime, as family members testified? (6) Had earlier domestic troubles in the Hossack house been resolved and all dissension ceased for over a year before the murder, as the family stated? and (7) Would it have been possible for an intruder or intruders to enter the house through the bedroom window, stand at the foot of the bed, and reach up to strike the fatal blows without rousing the woman who slept by her husband's side? An eighth question—what prompted Mrs. Hossack to leave home and wish her husband "out of the way"?—only entered the testimony twice. One neighbor, the wife of Mr. Haines, stated that she and her husband had come to aid Mrs. Hossack, who thought her husband would kill the family (Apr. 3). Another neighbor testified that he had to act as protector when Mrs. Hossack returned to her home "in case her husband again maltreated her as she had reason for believing" (Apr. 2).

Glaspell's reports do not suggest that the prosecution or the defense pursued the possibility of violence in the home, and she does not broach the subject herself. Instead, her stories of the trial tend to be summaries of testimony by experts and lay people who describe the structure of the brain, the disposition of the body in the bed, and the configuration of the blood spots on the walls. She does pause to describe the shock caused when the Hossack bed was brought into the courtroom, complete with bloodstained bedding, and when two vials of hairs were displayed—one found near the ax, the other obtained by exhuming John Hossack.

Interspersed between these accounts are her descriptions of the accused and of those attending the trial. During day one, for example, Glaspell describes Mrs. Hossack's reaction to the recital of counts against her: "Her eyes frequently filled with tears and her frame shook with emotion" (Apr. 2). On the next day, when the murder scene was again invoked, she notes that Mrs. Hossack, who occupied a seat by the sheriff's wife, surrounded by three of her daughters and all but one of her sons, broke down and wept bitterly: "Grief was not confined to her alone, it spread until the weeping group embraced the family and the sympathetic wife of Sheriff Hodson who frequently applied her handkerchief to her eyes" (Apr. 3).

Since there were no witnesses to the crime, the prosecution's case was based entirely on circumstantial evidence, and Glaspell often stops in her narration of testimony to weigh the success of the unsubstantiated arguments and to prod her readers to keep following the case. After one lengthy argument about how well Mrs. Hossack was able to wield an ax, Glaspell comments: "It must be admitted, however, that the prosecution has not thus far furnished any direct evidence and it is extremely doubtful if the chain of circumstantial evidence thus far offered will be sufficient to eliminate all doubt of the defendant's guilt from the minds of the jurors . . . on the other hand it is claimed by the prosecution attorney that the best evidence is yet to come" (Apr. 4). When Mrs. Hossack took the stand in her own defense and repeated the story she had held since the inquest, describing how she and her husband had spent a typical evening together the night of the crime—"He sat in the kitchen reading . . . later played with his whip . . . [while] I was patching and darning"—Glaspell observes, "When she left the stand, there seemed to be an impression on the audience that she had told the truth" (Apr. 8). Earlier questions of Mrs. Hossack's sanity apparently were dispelled by her composed appearance in court.

Like the novelist she would soon become, Glaspell saves her most impassioned descriptions for the climax of the trial, the summations by the lawyers. Of State Senator Berry, the defense counsel, she writes:

> It is said to be the master effort of his life . . . at times the jury without an exception was moved to tears. Strong men who had not shed a tear in years sat in their seats mopping their eyes and compressing their lips in a vain effort to suppress the emotion caused by the Senator's eloquent pleas. (Apr. 9)

This lachrymose display, she says, even extended to the prosecution attorneys, who were "seen to turn away their heads fearful lest the anguish of the family would unman them and the jury would have an impression which they could not afterward remove." The spectators were also moved. When the court was adjourned at noon, she writes, "fully two thousand people went out in the sunshine, their faces stained by the tears which had coursed down their cheeks."

Aside from tears Berry's chief strategy was to charge that Mr. Haines, "the insane man," was the real murderer. When he had been asked by the Hossack children to come to the house on the night of the murder, he had refused, saying that there were tramps about. It was he who had first implicated Mrs. Hossack by suggesting that she had wanted her husband dead and had sought his aid. And it was Mrs. Haines who had provided some of the most damning evidence about dissension in the Hossack home.

As successful as Berry may have been in concluding for the defense, Glaspell warns her readers that "it is certain that when attorney McNeal closes the argument for the prosecution the effect of Senator Berry's eloquence will have been lost and the verdict, if any at all is reached, can hardly be acquittal" (Apr. 9). Why, she does not say.

On the last day of the trial County Attorney Clammer and Mr. McNeal summarized for the prosecution, and, as Glaspell predicted, McNeal was able to rouse the audience with his indictment—"She did it, gentlemen, and I ask you to return it to her in kind . . . she has forfeited her right to live and she should be as John Hossack, who lies rotting beneath the ground." He, too, had his own bombshell: Margaret Hossack had been pregnant and given birth to a child before their marriage. This, McNeal claimed, was the dark secret often referred to in the trial, the story Hossack said he would take to his grave, and the reason for the unhappiness in the Hossack home. Just how a pregnancy thirty-three years earlier could have been the sole cause of trouble in the marriage and how it proved Mrs. Hossack's guilt in the murder of her husband was not clear, but, as Glaspell reports, it provided the jury with the impression that she was a woman who could not be trusted. It was with this revelation that the trial ended (Apr. 10).

The case went to the jury on April 10, the judge presenting the following charge: "When evidence consists of a chain of well authenticated circumstances, it is often more convincing and satisfactory and gives a stronger ground of assurance of the defendant's guilt than the direct testimony of witnesses unconfirmed by circumstances" (Apr. 11). In less than twenty-four hours the jury returned its verdict. Margaret Hossack was found guilty as charged and was sentenced to life imprisonment at hard labor. Glaspell reported the outcome but made no comment on the finding. It was the last story she filed in the case; it was also the last story she filed as a reporter for the *Des Moines Daily News*. Immediately after the trial she resigned and returned home to Davenport to begin writing fiction, and by the summer of 1901 she had moved to Chicago and enrolled in the graduate English program at the University of Chicago. Therefore, she may never have learned the final disposition of the Hossack case, for the story was not yet over. In April 1901 Lawyers Henderson and Berry lost an appeal with a lower court, but in April 1902 the Supreme Court of the State of Iowa agreed to hear the case. Citing several instances in which the trial judge had ruled incorrectly on the evidence, the higher court overturned the original conviction and requested a new trial.[3] A second trial took place in Madison County in February 1903. This time the jury, after twenty-seven hours of deliberation, was unable to reach a verdict: nine voting for conviction and three for acquittal. In papers filed in April 1903 the prosecutor stated that, since no further information had surfaced, if would be a waste of taxpayers' money to ask a third jury to hear the case. Mrs. Hossack, then near sixty and in failing health, was ordered released and was allowed to return to her home, her guilt or innocence still in question. . . .

Trifles begins at home. A murder has been committed—a man strangled while he slept—and his wife, who claimed to be sleeping beside him at the time, has been accused of the crime and been taken to jail to await trial. Those prosecuting the case, County Attorney Henderson and Sheriff Peters, have returned to the scene to search for clues that will provide "a motive; something to show anger, or—sudden feeling" and explain "the funny way" the man was murdered, "rigging it all up like that." Accompanying them are Mr. Hale, who found the body; Mrs. Peters, the sheriff's wife, charged with bringing the accused woman some of her things; and Mrs. Hale, who keeps her company in the kitchen below while the men move around the upstairs bedroom and perimeter of the farmhouse searching for clues.

In the absence of the wife the women, like quilters, patch together the scenario of her life and of her guilt. As they imagine her, Minnie Foster Wright is a lonely, childless woman, married to a taciturn husband, isolated from neighbors because of the rigors of farm life. When they discover a bird cage, its door ripped off and a canary, its neck wrung, they have no trouble making the connection. The husband has killed the bird, the wife's only comfort, as he killed the birdlike spirit of the woman. The motive and method of murder become as clear to them as the signs of sudden anger they infer from the half-wiped kitchen table and Minnie's erratic quilt stitching. Based on such circumstantial evidence, the women try the case, find the accused guilty, but dismiss the charge, recognizing the exigencies that led her to the act. In the process of judging they become compeers, Mrs. Peters recognizing her own disenfranchisement under the law and her own potential for violence, Mrs. Hale recognizing her failure to sustain her neighbor and thus her culpability in driving the desperate woman to kill.

This brief summary indicates how few specific details remain in Glaspell's re-visioning of the Hossack case. There is mention of "that man who went crazy," but he is not named or connected to the events.[4] Of the names of the participants only Henderson is used, assigned to the county attorney rather than the defense lawyer. Margaret Hossack has been renamed Minnie Foster Wright, the pun on the surname marking her lack of "rights" and implying her right to free herself against the societally sanctioned right of her husband to control the family, a right implicit in the Hossack case.

Glaspell's most striking alterations are her excision of Minnie and the change of venue. The accused woman has been taken away to jail before *Trifles* begins, her place signified by the empty rocking chair that remains in her kitchen. By not physically representing Minnie on the stage, the playwright is able to focus on issues that move beyond the guilt or innocence of one person. Since the audience never actually sees Minnie, it is not swayed by her person, but, instead, by her condition, a condition shared by other women who can be imagined in the empty subject position. And by situating her play in the kitchen not the court, in the private space in which Minnie lived rather than the public space in which she will be tried, Glaspell is able to offer the audience a composite picture of the life of Minnie Wright, Margaret Hossack, and countless women whose experiences were not represented in court because their lives were not deemed relevant to the adjudication of their cases. Most important in her shift of venue, Glaspell can focus on the central question never asked in the original Hossack case, that concerning the motives for murder: Why do women kill?

Motives are writ large in *Trifles*. The mise-en-scène suggests the harshness of Minnie's life. The house is isolated, "down in a hollow and you don't see the road"—dark, foreboding, a kind of rural, Gothic scene.

The interior of the kitchen replicates this barrenness and the commensurate disjunctions in the family, as the woman experienced them. Things are broken, cold, imprisoning; they are also violent. "Preserves" explode from lack of heat, a punning reminder of the causal relationship between isolation and violence. The mutilated cage and bird signify the brutal nature of Wright and the physical abuse the wife has borne. Employing expressionistic techniques, Glaspell externalizes Minnie's desperation and the conditions that caused it.[5] She also finds the dramatic correlative for revenge. Rather than use an ax, this abused wife strangles her husband: a punishment to fit his crime. So powerfully does Glaspell marshal the evidence of Minnie's strangled life that the jury on the stage and the jury who observe them from the audience presume the wife's right to take violent action in the face of the violence done to her. They see what might cause women to kill.

When Glaspell turns to the characters in her play she again reworks the figures from the Hossack case, offering a revisionary reading of their roles in the original trial. The lawmen in *Trifles* bear traces of the original investigators, the county attorney and the sheriff. Mr. Hale is Glaspell's invention, a composite of the Indianola farmers who testified at the Hossack trial, his name possibly derived from Mr. Haines. By introducing a man not directly charged with prosecution of the case, Glaspell is able to show a patriarchal power and privilege, the united front that judged Margaret Hossack. She also illustrates the process through which an individual joins the ranks.

In "A Jury of Her Peers" she goes to great lengths to indicate Mr. Hale's awkwardness at the beginning of the story, as he relates the details of the case, and how easily he is intimidated by the county attorney. Yet when he is allowed—by virtue of his gender—to go upstairs with the men of law, it is Hale, not they, who directly taunts the women: "But would the women know a clue if they did come upon it?" It is also he whom Glaspell ironically says speaks "with good natured superiority" when he declares that "women are used to worrying over trifles." Gender transcends class here, as it did in the original trial, in which the farmers, jurors, and lawyers had a common connection: they were male, and, as such, they were in control of the court and the direction of the testimony. She also indicates, however, that the privileged club does have a pecking order. Mr. Hale is recently admitted—or, more likely, only temporarily admitted—and, therefore, more likely to chide those below him in order to gain favor with those above. A similar desire to ingratiate themselves with the law and to establish a camaraderie that temporarily suspended class was clearly apparent among the farmers of Indianola, eager to play a part in convicting Mrs. Hossack, some so ready that their zeal in intruding themselves into the investigation was cited in the Supreme Court reversal.

Constructing her category of men across class lines, establishing their connectedness based on legal empowerment and rights, Glaspell summarily dismisses them to roam about on the periphery of the tale, their presence theatrically marked by shuffling sounds above the heads of the women and occasional appearances as they scurry out to the barn. With her deft parody Glaspell undercuts the authority they wielded in the original case and throws into question their sanctioned preserve of power. They physically crisscross the stage as they verbally crisscross the details of the crime, both actions leading nowhere, staged to show ineffectuality and incompetence.

In her version of the Hossack case it is the women, also drawn across class lines, who occupy their place, standing in stage center and functioning as the composite shaping consciousness that structures the play.[6] Glaspell carefully chooses the two women who will usurp legal agency. Mrs. Peters is the wife of the sheriff, patterned after Sheriff Hodson's wife, whose acts of kindness to Margaret Hossack seem to have stayed in Glaspell's memory. At first Mrs. Peters parrots the masculinist view and voice of her husband, defending the search of the home as men's "duty." She gradually comes to recognize, however, that marital designation— wife of the sheriff—offers her no more freedom than it does Minnie; in fact, it completely effaces her as an individual. Glaspell illustrates this condition by having the women identified only by their surnames, while, at the same time, they seek to particularize Minnie, referring to her by both her first and her maiden name.[7]

To the men, however, Minnie is John Wright's wife, just as Mrs. Peters is the sheriff's wife: "married to the law," "one of us," "not in need of supervision." Even Mrs. Hale, at the beginning of "Jury," assumes that Mrs. Peters will be an extension of her husband and will share his views of the murder. Yet as Mrs. Peters slowly ferrets out the facts of Minnie's life— the childlessness, the isolation—and conflates the experiences with her own early married days, she begins to identify with Minnie. It is when she comes upon the bird cage and the dead canary that she makes the most important connection: an understanding of female violence in the face of male brutality: "When I was a girl—my kitten—there was a boy took a hatchet, and before my eyes—and before I could get there—*(covers her face an instant)* If they hadn't held me back I would—*(catches herself, looks upstairs where steps are heard, falters weakly)*—hurt him."

It is significant that Glaspell attributes to Mrs. Peters, the sheriff's wife, the memory of a murder with an ax, the murder weapon in the Hossack case, and offers as sign of brutality the dismemberment of an animal, a trace, perhaps of the turkey in the original case. In the reversal of roles that Glaspell stages—in having Mrs. Peters act in lieu of her husband, dispensing her verdict based on her reading of the case and the motives for murder—she destroys the notion that a woman is her husband. She also stages what a woman may become when given legal power: a subject acting under her own volition, her decisions not necessarily coinciding with her husband's or with the male hegemony. She becomes self-deputized.

If Mrs. Peters is taken from life, so too is Mrs. Hale, a possible surrogate for the young reporter Susan Glaspell.[8] Just as Mrs. Peters recognizes her own potential for murder in the face of powerlessness, and this recognition motivates her to act and to seize the juridical position, Mrs. Hale comes to her own awareness in the course of the play. What she discovers in the kitchen of the Wright home is her own complicity in Minnie's situation, because of the aid she has withheld. "We live close together and we live far apart. We all go through the same thing, it's just a different kind of the same thing," she says, summarizing her insight about "how it is for women." In light of the Hossack case and Glaspell's role in sensationalizing the proceedings and in shaping public opinion, the lines appear to be confessional; thus, to her question "Who will punish that?" Mrs. Hale's words seem to indicate that Glaspell's awareness in 1916 of her omissions and commissions in 1901, of her failure to act in Margaret Hossack's behalf, and of her failure to recognize the implications of the trial for her own life.

Given this awareness, it may seem strange that, when Glaspell has the opportunity to retry Margaret Hossack and change the outcome of the case, she does not acquit the woman, or, as Kayann Short argues, give her "her day in court" (9) to prove her innocence. Instead, she has Mrs. Peters and Mrs. Hale assume Minnie's guilt and, as in the original trial, base their findings on circumstantial evidence instead of incontrovertible proof. When approaching *Trifles* in relation to the Hossack case, however, it becomes clear that acquittal is not Glaspell's intention, not why she wrote the play. Whether Margaret Hossack or Minnie Wright committed murder is moot; what is incontrovertible is the brutality of their lives, the lack of options they had to redress grievances or to escape abusive husbands, and the complete disregard of their plight by the courts and by society. Instead of arguing their innocence, Glaspell concretizes the conditions under which these women live and the circumstances that might cause them to kill. She thus presents the subtext that was excised from the original trial and that undergirds so many of the cases cited in Ann Jones's study: men's fears of women who might kill and women's fears of the murder they might be forced to commit. In so doing, she stages one of the first modern arguments for justifiable homicide.[9] By having Mrs. Peters and Mrs. Hale unequivocally assume Minnie's guilt and also assume justification for her act, Glaspell presents her audience/jury with a defense that forces it to confront the central issues of female powerlessness and disenfranchisement and the need for laws to address such issues.[10]

Yet Glaspell does not actually present the victimization of women or the violent acts such treatment may engender; instead, she stages the potential for female action and the usurpation of power.[11] By having the women assume the central positions and conduct the investigation and the trial, she actualizes an empowerment that suggests that there are options short of murder that can be imagined for women. Mrs. Peters and Mrs. Hale may seem to conduct their trial sub rosa because they do not actively confront the men, but in Mrs. Hale's final words, "We call it— knot it," ostensibly referring to a form of quilting but clearly addressed to the actions the women have taken, they become both actors and namers. Even if the men do not understand the pun—either through ignorance or, as Judith Fetterley suggests, through self-preservation—the audience certainly does. It recognizes that the women have achieved an important political victory: they have wrested control of language, a first step in political ascendancy, and they have wrested control of the case and the stage. Not waiting to be given the vote or the right to serve on juries, Glaspell's women have taken the right for themselves. Her audience in 1916 would get the point. It would also understand that Glaspell is deconstructing the very assumptions about the incontrovertibility of the law and about its absolutist position. Mrs. Peters and Mrs. Hale, by suturing into their deliberations their own experiences and fears—just as the men in the Hossack case did—illustrate the subjective nature of the reading of evidence and, by implication, of all essentialist readings.

In 1916 it would be clearer than it often is to contemporary audiences that Glaspell is more concerned with legal and social empowerment than with replacing one hierarchy with another; that women acting surreptitiously may be less a comment on their natures than on the political systems that breed such behavior; not that women speak "in a different voice" but, rather, that they speak in a manner deriving from their different position under the law, from their common erasure. Her depiction of the con-

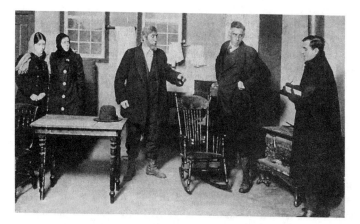

The Provincetown Players' 1917 production of Susan Glaspell's *Trifles*

ditions of her women is close to what Catherine MacKinnon describes in her book *Feminism Unmodified*: women's actions—their voices—deriving not from some innate nature but from the ways they have been forced to speak and to act. MacKinnon suggests that, if legal and social changes could occur, it would then be time to decide how a woman "talks."[12] When women are powerless, she argues, "you don't just speak differently. A lot, you don't speak. Your speech is not differently articulated, it is silenced" (39). In *Trifles* Glaspell, like MacKinnon, posits gender as a production of the inequality of power under law, "a social status based on who is permitted to do what to whom" (MacKinnon 8). . . .

At the time she wrote *Trifles* Glaspell was living in a community passionately concerned with socialism and feminism; she herself was a founding member of Heterodoxy, the New York–based group of women whose numbers included activists Marie Jenny Howe, Crystal Eastman, Elizabeth Irwin, Mary Heaton Vorse, and, for a time, Charlotte Perkins Gilman.[13] The audience for the Provincetown Players was already a body of the committed, who in 1916 worked for suffrage and for social reform that would redress class distinctions in the United States and who, for the most part, were opposed to Wilson and the war. Unlike many suffragists, their arguments were usually posited on a materialist rather than an essentialist reading of gender, concerned either with class struggles of which gender limitations were part or enlightenment ideals of individualism applicable to both women and men. They did not romanticize femininity; most debunked the "cult of the home." Their major concern was in insuring "that women shall have the same right as man to be different, to be individuals, not merely a social unit," and that this individualism would manifest itself in legal and social freedom.[14] It was for this audience and at this time that Glaspell returned to the Hossack case.

Trifles, therefore, is grounded in a double-focused historical context: the Iowa of 1901 and the Provincetown of 1916, the two periods leaving traces and providing many of the tensions and fissures that produce the contemporary feel to Glaspell's best works. Thus positioned, her writing acts as a palimpsest for the shifting roles of women in the early twentieth century and for her own shifts in attitudes toward the possibilities for women and herself. It is either a testament to the skill with which Glaspell constructed *Trifles* and "A Jury of Her Peers" or proof of how little women's lives have changed since 1916 that contemporary feminist critics still use the play and story as palimpsests for their own readings of contemporary feminist issues, and these readings still point to some of the dilemmas that faced Glaspell and her personae in 1901 and in 1916: how to free women from the stereotypic roles into which they have been cast, how to articulate their lives and their rights without reinscribing them in the very roles against which they inveigh, how to represent female power not victimization—in short, how to represent Margaret Hossack. Yet in reading the works through a contemporary grid, critics should be careful of turning them into contemporary tracts, assuming that, just because Glaspell offers a picture of two women who bond, she is arguing for a higher moral ground for women, romanticizing femininity and home, arguing sexual difference, or the categorization of women under a fixed moral genus.[15] Given her own interests and concerns at the time, and her own relation to the Hossack case, it is more likely that her play and story are illustrating the need to provide both male and female voices in court—and in art—if human experience is not to be forever subsumed under the male pronoun and if women's voices are to be heard not as difference but as equally registered.

NOTES

1. At the turn of the century the father of modern criminology, Cesare Lombroso, offered a checklist of the physical qualities that would identify women who might kill: "approximate more to males . . . than to normal women, especially in the superciliary arches in the seam of sutures, in the lower jaw-bones, and in peculiarities of the occipital region" (Jones 6).
2. The Hossack case was not unique in the number of women in attendance. Jones offers examples of irate ministers commenting on the large numbers of women who attended celebrated murder trials around the same period. In one case a min-

ister comments that, "It is a strange thing that women, under no compulsion whatever, are found in large numbers in every notorious trial everywhere, and the dirtier the trial the more woman usually will be found in attendance" (138). He does not conjecture about this phenomenon.

3. There were seven procedural points upon which the Supreme Court of Iowa based its reversal, the most significant of which were the following: that the hairs found under the corn crib were not proved to be from the murder weapon and had been taken by the county attorney and given to the sheriff and could not, therefore, be introduced as evidence; that the dissension in the Hossack house had abated at least a year prior to the murder and could not, therefore, be introduced in the case. See *State v. Hossack*, Supreme Court of Iowa, April 9, 1902, *Northwestern Reporter*, 1077–81.

4. See Hedges for a discussion of insanity in rural American life and the practice by women on the plains of having canaries to provide them company.

5. Glaspell often used expressionistic techniques in her plays. See Ben-Zvi, "Susan Glaspell and Eugene O'Neill" (1982 and 1986), for a discussion of *The Verge* as an expressionistic drama.

6. Mrs. Peters and Mrs. Hale are of different classes, a fact visually captured by the filmmaker Sally Heckel in her version of "A Jury of Her Peers" (Texture Films). Mrs. Hale wears a plain, cloth coat and head scarf; Mrs. Peters has a fur tippet and large, feathered hat.

Their language also bears signs of their class, a technique Glaspell often repeats. In *Trifles* Mrs. Hale makes grammatical errors, has unfinished sentences, drops letters. Mrs. Peters speaks in a grammatically correct manner befitting the sheriff's wife. For example, Mrs. Hale's comment, "I wonder if she was goin' to quilt it or just knot it" becomes Mrs. Peters's "We think she was going to—knot it," the omitted *g* signifying for Glaspell different education and position. What joins them is the men's categorization of them, predicated on gender, erasing difference, dismissing individuality.

7. At the time Glaspell was writing the play, the question of women taking their husbands' names was a political issue. One of Glaspell's friends, Ruth Hale, launched a movement called the Lucy Stone League, which supported married women who chose to keep their maiden names. (See Schwarz 14, 58, 83.) Glaspell, like her contemporaries Neith Boyce, Mary Heaton Vorse, and others, never assumed her husband's name.

8. When the Provincetown Players staged the play Glaspell chose to play Mrs. Hale and had her husband, George Cram Cook, play Hale.

9. One could argue that the precedent for staging a case of justifiable homicide for women was established in *The Oresteia*, in which the motives leading to Clytemnestra's murder of Agamemnon are delineated, or would be if one affixed to the work the murder of Iphigenia, as Ariane Mnouchkine did in a production of the Aeschylus' trilogy at the Théâtre du Soleil that is prefaced by Euripides' *Iphigenia in Aulis*. (See *New York Times*, March 27, 1981, B3, for a description of this performance.) For a discussion of contemporary wife battering cases and the plea of justifiable homicide, see Jones (chap. 6).

10. In most of Glaspell's plays there is a political component directly connected to particular events of her period that would have been immediately evident to her audience but is often lost in contemporary discussions of her works. In *Suppressed*

Desires, for instance, she takes on a noted antifeminist of the period, one Professor Sedwick, who had said, "All women were hens." In the play Glaspell and Cook play on the name Stephen (Step-hen), parodying both Freudianism and Cook's childhood pronunciation of the word (*Road* 25). Yet they are also answering Sedwick, a reference her audience would immediately have understood. Even more overtly, *Inheritors* challenges contemporary issues such as the Alien and Sedition laws and the Red Scare.

11. See Butler on the problems of staging victimization and thus representing the very condition the writer may wish to dismantle.

12. MacKinnon, while acknowledging the work of such people as Carol Gilligan, argues that Gilligan "achieves for moral reasoning what the special protection rule achieves in law: the affirmative rather than the negative valuation of that which has accurately distinguished women from men, by making it seem as though those attributes, with their consequences, really are somehow ours, rather than what male supremacy has attributed to us for its own use": "For women to affirm difference, when difference means dominance, as it does with gender, means to affirm the qualities and characteristics of powerlessness" (38–39). What is relevant about MacKinnon in relation to *Trifles* and "Jury" is her emphasis on law and enfranchisement. Reading Glaspell through MacKinnon allows the critics to move beyond the questions of "different voice" that were the critical bulwarks of the first moment of Glaspell criticism (see, e.g., Ben-Zvi, Stein, Alkalay-Gut, and Malpede) or critiqued in the more recent materialist readings (see Carroll, Hart, Nelligan [in *Susan Glaspell*], Short, Stephens, and Williams). It is hard to imagine, however, that Glaspell would have supported MacKinnon's stance on censorship as a way of alleviating pornography. Repeatedly in her writing, Glaspell objected to any form of censorship, for whatever reason.

13. See Judith Schwarz's description of Heterodoxy, in which she lists Glaspell as a founding member; also see Nancy Cott's detailed study of the feminist movement in New York in the years 1910–1920; and June Sochen's descriptions of the period and of Glaspell's relation to feminists in Greenwich Village. In *Women and American Socialism, 1870–1920* Buhle discusses how Glaspell "created female characters as working-class women with capacities to feel intensely, to understand injustice rather than internalizing oppression, and when conditions allowed to strike back at their oppressors" (203).

14. These quotations are taken from the same *New York Times* report (February 18, 1914) concerning a meeting organized by Heterodoxy president, Marie Jenny Howe, at Cooper Union, billed as "the first feminist meeting ever convened." At the time Glaspell was in Davenport, after suffering a miscarriage, but many of her friends were there, and she would most likely have been in the audience, if not on the dais. For other references to articles on feminism written between 1913–16, see Cott.

15. Five years later she would write *The Verge*, her most powerful and feminist play. Her persona, Claire Archer, would demand a life not circumscribed by the traditional roles assigned to women—mother, caregiver, hostess—and would stand in juxtaposition to her daughter and her sister, who represent conventional women whose gender does not provide them with an insight into Claire's life or her aspiration. In *The Verge* Glaspell also pursues feminism as a "transvaluation of values" on a Nietzschean model. See Cott (296) in relation to Dora Marsden and a similar position; also see Carroll.

WORKS CITED

Alkalay-Gut, Karen. " 'A Jury of Her Peers': The Importance of Trifles."
   Studies in Short Fiction 21 (1984): 3–11.
Barlow, Judith, ed. Plays by American Women: 1900–1930. New York:
   Applause Books, 1985.
Ben-Zvi, Linda. "Susan Glaspell and Eugene O'Neill." Eugene O'Neill
   Newsletter 6 (1982): 22–29.
———. "Susan Glaspell, Eugene O'Neill, and the Imagery of Gender."
   Eugene O'Neill Newsletter 10 (1986): 22–28.
———. "Susan Glaspell's Contributions to Contemporary Women Play-
   wrights." In Feminine Focus: The New Women Playwrights. Ed.
   Enoch Brater. New York: Oxford University Press, 1989. 147–66.
Bigsby, C. W. E., ed. Plays by Susan Glaspell. Cambridge: Cambridge Uni-
   versity Press, 1987.
Buhle, Mari Jo. Women and American Socialism, 1870–1920. Urbana:
   University of Illinois Press, 1981.
Butler, Judith. "Performing Acts and Gender Constitution: An Essay in
   Phenomenology and Feminist Theory." In Performing Feminisms:
   Feminist Critical Theory and Theatre. Ed. Sue-Ellen Case. Balti-
   more: Johns Hopkins University Press, 1990. 270–82.
Carroll, Kathleen. "Centering Women Onstage: Susan Glaspell's Dialogic
   Strategy of Resistance." PhD diss. University of Maryland, 1990.
Cott, Nancy. The Grounding of Modern Feminism. New Haven: Yale Uni-
   versity Press, 1987.
Gilligan, Carol. In a Different Voice: Psychological Theory and Women's
   Development. Cambridge: Harvard University Press, 1982.
Glaspell, Susan. "The Hossack Case." Des Moines Daily News, December
   2, 1900–April 13, 1901.
———. "A Jury of Her Peers." Everyweek, March 5, 1917.
———. Trifles. New York: Frank Shay/Washington Square Players, 1916;
   rpt. in Bigsby.
Hedges, Elaine. "Small Things Reconsidered: Susan Glaspell's 'A Jury of
   Her Peers.' " Women's Studies 12 (1986): 89–110.
Heilbrun, Carolyn. Writing a Woman's Life. New York: W. W. Norton, 1988.
Jones, Ann. Women Who Kill. New York: Holt, Rinehart and Winston,
   1980.
Kolodny, Annette. "A Map for Re-Reading: Gender and the Interpretation
   of Literary Texts." In The New Feminist Criticism. Ed. Elaine
   Showalter. New York: Pantheon, 1985. 46–62.

Larabee, Ann. "Death in Delphi: Susan Glaspell and the Companionate Marriage." Mid-American Review 7, no. 2 (1987): 93–106.

MacKinnon, Catherine. Feminism Unmodified: Discourses on Life and Law. Cambridge: Harvard University Press, 1987.

Malpede, Karen. "Introduction." Women in Theatre. New York: Drama Books, 1983.

Murphy, Jeanette. "A Question of Silence." In Films for Women. Ed. Charlotte Brunsdon. London: British Film Institute, 1986. 99–108.

Noe, Marcia. Susan Glaspell: Voice from the Heartland. Macomb: Western Illinois Monograph Series, 1983.

Northwestern Reporter, April 9, 1902: 1077–81.

Polk County Transcripts of Court Records, case no. 805, April 2, 1901–March 3, 1903.

Rockwell, John. "An Oresteia Using Non-Western Techniques." New York Times. March 27, 1981.

Schwarz, Judith. Radical Feminists of Heterodoxy: Greenwich Village, 1912–1940. Lebanon, N.H.: New Victoria Publishers, 1982.

Short, Kayann. "A Different Kind of the Same Thing: The Erasure of Difference in 'A Jury of Her Peers.'" In Trifles and "A Jury of Her Peers" Casebook. Ed. Linda Ben-Zvi, forthcoming.

Sochen, June. The New Woman in Greenwich Village, 1910–1920. New York: Quadrangle, 1972.

Stein, Karen. "The Women's World of Glaspell's Trifles." In Women in American Theatre. Ed. Helen Krich Chinoy and Linda Walsh Jenkins. New York: Theatre Communications Group, 1987. 253–56.

Stephens, Judith. "Gender Ideology and Dramatic Convention in Progressive Era Plays, 1890–1920." In Performing Feminisms: Feminist Critical Theory and Theatre. Ed. Sue-Ellen Case. Baltimore: Johns Hopkins University Press, 1990. 283–93.

Supreme Court of Iowa, April 9, 1902, Northwestern Reporter: 1077–81.

"Talk on Feminism Stirs Great Crowd." New York Times, February 18, 1914.

Warren County Court Records. Hossack trial, April 1903.

Williams, Linda. "A Jury of Their Peers: Marlene Gorris's 'A Question of Silence.'" In Postmodernism and Its Discontents: Theories and Practices. Ed. E. Ann Kaplan. London: Verso, 1988. 107–15.

KAREN ALKALAY-GUT

Murder and Marriage: Another Look at *Trifles*

The objective plot of Glaspell's most successful play, *Trifles*, is very much at odds with the triviality of the title.[1] The story is of the brutal murder by a wife of her husband, the evidence for which is covered up by other women almost unaquainted with the perpetrator. When even a sheriff's wife is willing to become an accessory after the fact to a murder because she seems to agree to its inevitability, it is necessary to ask some basic questions: What is it that the women perceive to have in common that necessitates this bond, and what do audiences generations after have in common with these women that this decision is accepted as inescapable?

It is certainly not the fidelity to truth that encourages identification. Some of the elements of the play were drawn from contemporary reality, but the others that were altered were basic. When Susan Glaspell covered the case of Margaret Hossack, who was charged with killing her husband with an ax while he was asleep in December, 1900, she discovered the inconsistency of the legal system that excluded women from judicial decisions but judged them nevertheless. It was not only Glaspell who found herself drawn to this case: the trial drew a crowd of up to two thousand people. But despite the many parallels in the case, including the "sympathetic wife of Sheriff Hodson," who sat with Margaret Hossack throughout the trial, in reality Hossack was convicted in her first trial.

Glaspell's need to change the ending of the trial, to empower women to rectify an apparently unjust situation, is both a criticism of the legal system and an indictment of the social and romantic conventions of society. The danger to women is not only in the legal system but also for those who do not run afoul of the law, in the very structure of marriage. Women, in the context of *Trifles* and even more in the story "A Jury of Her Peers," are trapped by a social system that may lead them into crime and punish them when they are forced to commit it. It is this situation of the double bind with which the women of the play identify and which readers and audiences continue to explore. "We all go through the same things—it's all just a different kind of the same thing" (*Trifles* 26–27), Mrs. Hale tells Mrs. Peters in the play and adds in the story: "If it weren't—why do you and I *understand*? Why do we *know*—what we know this minute?" ("Jury" 86)

The typical romantic background for the brutal murder is not explained onstage, but one need only examine the name of the protagonist, Minnie Foster, to understand its integrality with what goes on in the dreary farmhouse. The name Minnie is derived from the German word for *love*; this potential for love is nurtured and cherished in Minnie's maiden name, Foster; when she discovers her ideal man, Mr. Wright (Right), it is transferred to her husband. Mrs. Wright is then an emblematic romantic heroine of standard tales for women, whose potential is "fulfilled" through the right man, when she becomes acceptable as "Mrs. Right." Mrs. Hale and Mrs. Peters, the other women in the play, have also followed this pattern, fulfilling themselves as "wives" of men—and it is only in this capacity, as wives of the witness and of the sheriff, that they are invited to be present at the investigation at all.

As the emblematic woman, Mrs. Wright's own life becomes, of necessity, trivial. Her absence throughout the play emphasizes this tangentiality to existence. But it is also apparent in the position of the other women, who have, as Christine Dymkowski has pointed out, been confined to the least significant room of the house, the kitchen, for the duration of the investigation. And even that kitchen is available to the women only when it is vacated by the men. When the women remain by the door until the men leave, "the separateness of the female and male world is . . . immediately established visually and then reinforced by the dialogue" (Dymkowski 92).

For the significant world is elsewhere: the men search for clues in the barn, in the bedroom, in higher spheres—"upstairs"—and in the world outside the farmhouse, and they allow the women in the kitchen no relevance. The women are present only to collect Minnie Wright's trivial and unaccountably needed paraphernalia for her stay in jail. The apron that Mrs. Wright requests—irrelevant to her prison activities yet essential to her concept of self as practical and protected servant—would only be a further source of derision to the men, who are far too ready to laugh at any woman's request, even those that might appear to make sense. Not only Mrs. Wright's concern for the jars of fruit that might freeze in the unheated kitchen but also Mrs. Hale's apprehension about leaving her work undone and her curiosity about Mrs. Wright's sewing are at best causes for impatience on the part of the men.

And yet, of course, it is precisely their unwillingness to perceive the potential relevance of the kitchen, the world and pattern of the women, that excludes the men from understanding what has happened: they fail to comprehend the motivations for the events, and the method of uncovering the underlying pattern eludes them. The little squares of material being formed into a quilt that the women decide to bring to Mrs. Wright to "occupy her time" are ridiculed by the men but provide an unrecognized key to this male exclusion because this quilting method parallels the only ways clues could form the truth: the joining together of scraps of details allows the women to comprehend the situation of Minnie Foster and her development from housewife to criminal. The "log cabin" patchwork the women discover in Minnie Foster's sewing basket is made exactly in this fashion: rectangular strips are sewn around the original square or rectangle, followed by a series of longer scraps, which are measured to the increasing size of the patch. Each patch has an individual entity, but its beauty (and meaning) is in relationship to the other patches formed with similar painstaking consideration. The colors are coordinated and contrasted by balance and relationship, but the general pattern is one that emerges with the quilt.

The significant world for the men is elsewhere, but for the women it is in the ordering of the scraps of information around the central "square" of marriage and the total dependence of the wife upon her husband for all physical, emotional, and spiritual fulfillment as well as validation as a human being. The shabbiness of the clothes that Mrs. Wright requests for her stay in jail, the broken rocker and the bad stove in the kitchen indicate John Wright's "stinginess," his unwillingness to provide basic warmth and shelter for his wife. Wright's objection to a telephone, Mr. Hale's initial reason for his visit and the reason for his discovery of the crime, is unquestionably further deterrence on the part of the husband to his wife's communication with the world and validation as an individual.

It is because she realizes that these details don't count to the men that her communication with the outside world will be deemed irrelevant, that Minnie Foster can retell her story with many particulars, the significance of which she can be certain will escape her interrogators. When asked about her husband's murder she explains, "He died of a rope round his neck." In retrospect it becomes clear that her explanation reflects her vision of the murder as a symbolic retribution, a revenge execution for the strangling of her canary (in itself a symbolic act).

Yet this is not all that Minnie explains in these lines. The physical complexity of this method of murder is apparent to Mrs. Peters, the sheriff's wife, who in the play puzzles, "They say it was such a—funny way to kill a man, rigging it all up like that" (*Trifles* 21), leaving the reader to interpret the action. For to Minnie this is an administered death and not a murder, and the husband is not a "victim" but, instead, dies as one would die of a long chronic illness, "of a rope around his neck." Mr. Hale, the one man who is not totally alienated from the world of women, seems momentarily to grasp the significance. "It looked . . . ," begins Mr. Hale, in both the story and the play, but is overcome by emotion and cannot continue, because this particular method of murder not only recalls the woman next to him in bed to whom he too is bound but also the situation of marriage in general, in which the couple are bound together; and marriage for the husband is popularly referred to as a noose. Mrs. Wright's further description elaborates on this relationship: "Weren't you sleepin' in the bed with him?" Mrs. Hale's son, the only unmarried character, asks her. " 'Yes,' says she, 'but I was on the inside.' " Spatially, the couple slept in the same bed and should have defended each other against the world outside, but because the woman was "on the inside," in the protected and passive position, she claims to have been rendered helpless and even unconscious. Since the primary differences between men and women are described in spatial terms like this throughout the play as well as the story, with the "significant" events repeatedly placed on the outside and the "trivial" on the inside,[2] this detail is crucial and foreshadows the affected innocence of the wives at the end.

"If I am given no power," Minnie Foster seems to say, "then how can I claim to have any?" How can she claim to have murdered her husband if she has always been on the "inside," where important things don't happen, and, if she has always been thought to know only trivia, why should she now claim to have known more? The women accept this premise and base their final decision on the same premises. Relegated to the kitchen, they do not point out that it is, ultimately, the most significant room in the house. Reduced to poking through a sewing kit while the men look for important clues, they do not reveal that in this inner sanctum is the secret that could validate the men's case.

This behavior alone does not simply illustrate the generally accepted feminist message that women must stick together. As Karen Stein argues: "The women here realize, through their involvement in the murder investigation, that only by joining together can they, isolated and insignificant in their society, obtain for themselves and extend to others the support and sympathy that will help them endure the loneliness and unceasing labor required of them."[3] Underlying Stein's attitude is the assumption that the women's lives are individually trivial and that their only strength and/or success can come from banding together. Triviality can be overcome by the unification of large numbers, by sewing together the scraps into a quilt.

There are two important problems with this assertion. First, it is only in the most limited sense that the women's lives can be seen to be occupied with trivia. And second, what brings the women together, what forces them to endanger themselves for a criminal, is the fact that they do not only sympathize but also *identify* with the murderess.

Trivia, the concerns of life that are weighed as insignificant when compared to more central and weighty interests, begin the story, although not the play. Mrs. Hale is compelled to leave her own kitchen, where she has been engaged in sifting flour, in order to participate in a murder investigation. But she finds the decision difficult to make: "It was no ordinary thing that called her away—it was probably farther from ordinary than anything that had ever happened in Dickson County. But what her eye took in was that her kitchen was in no shape for leaving: her bread all ready for mixing, half the flour sifted and half unsifted" ("Jury" 70). The kitchen is a world of simple imperatives—cleanliness, order, productivity, economy, and fruitfulness. Mrs. Hale's dilemma in leaving her kitchen might suggest her lack of hierarchy in values, her "typically feminine" concern for insignificant details, but although she keeps the investigators waiting out in the sleigh while she contemplates this scene, it is the contemplation that allows her later to comprehend the urgency of Minnie Foster's actions, for Mrs. Hale, like Mrs. Wright, was impelled by a "chill wind" to abandon the making of bread.

The detail assumes centrality, then, when the "important" clues fade, lead in the wrong direction, and/or disappear. This is something Mrs. Hale learns when the county attorney criticizes the dirty towel in the Wright kitchen. "Not much of a housekeeper, would you say Ladies?" he asks rhetorically, both in the play and story, and Mrs. Hale feels moved to defend Mrs. Wright on the basis of her sympathy with the difficult life of farm wives, while accepting his conclusion from the evidence. Later, when her evaluations have assumed different proportions, she understands that the attorney's deduction was based upon the necessity to integrate the perceived details with the assumption of Minnie's guilt and her accompanying inevitable character flaw as a woman.[4] At that point she can release her observations from his psychological imperatives and realize that the towel is dirty because the deputy had wiped his hands on it when he made the fire.

For the men details, then, are not trivial but become integrated into the male preexisting vision. The trivial minutiae in themselves cannot be examined because they are not conceived of as separate from a larger fabric, a more general theory, clues to support a thesis. It is this limitation that prevents the men from understanding the murder case, and it [is] this same limitation that prevents them from comprehending their wives' situation, which in turn forces the wives to employ passivity and subterfuge. Mr. Hale, increasingly influenced by the demeaning attitude of the other men toward the women, asks "Would the women know a clue if they did come on it?" unaware that the approach of the women has been far more productive and also of the fact that his attitude has made it impossible for his wife to share vital information with him. His silence for the rest of the play is an indication of his inaccessibility to the women.[5]

The initial discriminatory division between the men and women of the play becomes one of choice. Women band together to protect one another from the evaluations of men because the men are simply not capable of understanding their situation, the same situation that led to the murder in the first place; and it is a political as well as a social condition.

The political nature of the situation is made clear by the title of the story, "A Jury of Her Peers." Elizabeth Cady Stanton, in her address to the Legislature of the State of New York on February 14, 1854, used the term first:

> The most sacred of all rights, trial by a jury of our own peers. . . . [S]hall an erring woman be dragged before a bar of grim-visaged judges, lawyers, and jurors, there to be grossly questioned in public on subjects which most women scarce breathe in secret to one another? Shall the most sacred relations of life be called up and rudely scanned by men who, by their own admission, are so coarse that women could not meet them even at the polls without contamination? [And] yet shall she find there no woman's face or voice to pity and defend? Shall the frenzied mother, who to save herself and child from exposure and disgrace, ended the life that had but just begun, be dragged before such a tribunal to answer for her crime? How can man enter into the feelings of that mother?[6]

When *Trifles* and "A Jury of Her Peers" were written, women in the state of Iowa did not have the right of which Stanton spoke. Women served in juries only in Utah, Washington, Kansas, and California (Kerber 16). Suffrage, of course, was in the future. This disenfranchisement makes inevitable a different perspective on justice and the concept of primary responsibility to the law. "The law is the law," Mrs. Peters first asserts, in the story version but not in *Trifles*, horrified by her gradual revelation that there may be something other than the law, and Mrs. Hale soon adds: "The law is the law—and a bad stove is a bad stove." The law just does not apply here—because women have nothing to say in matters that concern women and because the scale of values is simply different for men and women. Carol Gilligan has pointed out that this distinction is seen as a flaw in women's judgment. Freud, writing at the same time as Glaspell, noted that "for women the level of what is ethically normal is different from what it is in men . . . [and] concluded that women 'show less sense of justice than men, that they are less ready to submit to the great exigencies of life, that they are more often influenced in their judgment by feelings of affection or hostility' " (Gilligan 7).

My point here is that the problem is far more complex than that of loyalty to women rather than to men. Legally, the women who protect Minnie Wright are criminals, accessories after the fact, guilty of concealing evidence. If the legal system is right (Wright) then their crimes are plainly wrong, their sympathies allowing them (as often is the case with women in stereotypical situations, according to Freud and others) to ignore the higher significance of their actions as they allow their emotions to take over. The gradual process in which this incipient "criminality" develops could help to prove this argument. For as Weisbrod points out, the women progress in their deception from concealment to a lie. Beginning with the fruit that has been spoiled because the fire in the faulty stove went out (another obvious symbol of the thwarted fruition of Mrs. Wright's life due to an absence of warmth), when Mrs. Hale says: "If I was you I wouldn't *tell* her her fruit was gone! Tell her it ain't. . . . here—take this [the one surviving jar] to prove it to her!" (*Trifles* 27), the progression is from concealment to a lie to, finally, a truth put forward to prove a lie, so that the woman in jail will not be further injured by the knowledge that her fruit has been ruined. "This scene anticipates the women's concealing the evidence" (Weisbrod 78 n. 67). Indeed, from lying about the fruit they move to a lie about the murder.

It is, however, only when they realize that the men are not capable of understanding the evidence before them, when they realize that there is no chance of a fair trial, that they resort to these deceptions. These are not deceptions of weakness or of emotions and sisterhood overriding logic and morality. They are calculated deceits that are only perpetrated upon those who have proven themselves blind to the clues, insensitive to the trivia that delineate the lives of all women in the play, including Minnie Foster. For not only do all women share the loneliness of housewifery, each woman alone in her own house, not only do the women feel the potential for violence on the part of the men in their lives (as does Mrs. Peters, remembering her kitten playfully slaughtered like Mrs. Wright's canary), but they all suffer from the unwillingness or inability of the men to understand their situation of helpless isolation, their constrained passivity, their overwhelming enforced dependence. Mrs. Peters and Mrs. Hale know that, like Mrs. Wright, their identities, their lives, and their futures have been determined totally by the men they have married. Mrs. Hale's fortune is better than the rest, perhaps, and Mrs. Peters has been enlisted, by marriage, into a stable system of justice with which she need not argue. But had the situation been different, either of these women might have been in Mrs. Wright's bed and compelled to murder the man whose total control over her was, in this case, totally negative. "If they hadn't held me back," says Mrs. Peters, remembering her slaughtered kitten, "I would have—(*Catches herself, looks upstairs where steps are heard, falters weakly)*—hurt him" (*Trifles* 26). In this situation, in which the individual is not free to make decisions, to determine the consequences of actions, the legal concept of justice is simply not relevant. What would be murder to a free agent is here tyrannicide and/or justified revolution. The emotional responsibility of Mr. Wright to provide for his wife's needs was ignored by him and would be ignored by any all-male jury.

And yet the concluding scene is one of total feminine community, symbolized by the work of quilting. Not only is quilting a simple communal task in which the trivial becomes integrated vitally into a larger framework, but it also makes use of hidden patterns and significances. To quilt a blanket is to sew the joined patches to the lining all the way around the borders of the patch. It is to make a thin, flat quilt, in which all the thicknesses are equal. To know a quilt is to sew the fabric together, generally through a thicker lining, only at the corners of each patch. Quilting equalizes the thickness of the blanket; knotting emphasizes the distinctions. When the women inform the men at the conclusion that Minnie was planning to knot the quilt, although they had not discussed this matter between them, they determine to differentiate between the legal definition of the crime, in which all considerations external to the act itself are meaningless and equal, and their moral definition of the crime, in which nothing is even and flat. Distinctions must be made, with the delicacy of a needle, and they have made them.

Patchworking is conceived as a collective activity, for, although it is the individual woman who determines the patterns, collects and cuts the scraps, and pieces them together, quilting work on an entire blanket is too arduous for a single person. Minnie's patchwork would have been knotted and not quilted because knotting is easier and can be worked alone. And the guilty-hearted Mrs. Hale knows this.

With her hand against the pocket of her coat, where the bird is hidden, Mrs. Hale emphasizes the additional meanings of the phrase "knot it"— meanings she is certain her investigators will overlook, as they have overlooked every other significant fact. "Knot it" conveys the sense of knotting the rope around the husband's neck: the women disclose the murderess. But they will "knot" tell. Mrs. Hale speaks a language understood now by Mrs. Peters but totally incomprehensible to those who cannot perceive the significance of trifles.

If the women "trifle" with the evidence, it is with the full recognition that they are meting out a different form of justice, the justice of women, the justice of those whose case could not be understood by anyone unwilling to proceed from details to an unprejudiced understanding of the truth.

NOTES

1. I am particularly grateful to Aviam Soifer, Dean, Boston College Law School, who first helped me to see the legal issues of this play.
2. For an elaboration of this concept, see my article: "'A Jury of Her Peers': The Importance of *Trifles*," *Studies in Short Fiction* (Winter 1984): 1–9.
3. Karen Stein, "The Women's World of Glaspell's *Trifles*," *Women in American Theatre*, ed. Helen Krich Chinoy and Linda Walsh Jenkins (New York: Crown, 1981), 251–54.
4. The prevalent belief about women who murder at the time of this play seems to have been that only a depraved woman could murder. If a depraved person sins against society somehow, the fault lies in his or her mind, but, when a "normal" socialized person commits a murder, there is an implied criticism of society. Therefore it is necessary for the county attorney to understand Minnie as deviant as a housewife. This, of course, explains the general masculine criticism of Mrs. Wright's housekeeping as well as the attempts to perceive Mrs. Wright as out of her mind.
5. Speaking as a sign of empowerment has been noted and discussed by Marijane Camilleri, "Lessons in Law from Literature: A Look at the Movement and a Peer in Her Jury," *Catholic University Law Review* 39 (1990): 588. The effect on the stage is the women's silence in the presence of the men, and, of course, the overwhelming pervasive silence of Minnie Wright.
6. I am indebted to note 46 in the article by Carol Weisbrod, "Images of the Woman Juror," *Harvard Women's Law Journal* 9 (1986): 59–82, for pointing out this passage. Elizabeth Cady Stanton's address has been reprinted in *History of Woman Suffrage, 1848–1861*, ed. E. C. Stanton, S. B. Anthony, and M. J. Gage, 2d. ed., (New York: Arno Press, 1969): 595–98. Lucy Stone also used this phrase in an even more relevant context, pleading for a fair trial for Lizzie Borden ("A Flaw in the Jury System," *Women's Journal* [June 17, 1893]: 188).

WORKS CITED

Camilleri, Marijane. "Lessons in Law from Literature: A Look at the Movement and a Peer in Her Jury," Catholic University Law Review 39 (1990): 557–94.

Des Moines Daily News. 14 Jan. 1901.

Dymkowski, Christine. "On the Edge: The Plays of Susan Glaspell." Modern Drama 31 (1988): 91–105.

Gilligan, Carol. In a Different Voice. Cambridge: Harvard University Press, 1982.

Glaspell, Susan. "A Jury of Her Peers." The Wadsworth Casebook Series for Reading, Research, and Writing: Trifles. Ed. Donna Winchell. Boston: Wadsworth, 2004. 70–88.

Glaspell, Susan. Trifles. The Wadsworth Casebook Series for Reading, Research, and Writing: Trifles. Ed. Donna Winchell. Boston: Wadsworth, 2004. 15–28.

Kerber, Linda. "The Case of the Broken Baseball Bat: Women and the Obligation of Jury Service. Hoyt v. Florida 368 U.S. 57 (1961)." Ms.

Stein, Karen. "The Women's World of Susan Glaspell's Trifles." Women in American Theatre. ed. Helen Krich Chinoy and Linda Walsh Jenkins. New York: Crown, 1981. 251–254.

Weisbrod, Carol. "Images of the Woman Juror." Harvard Women's Law Journal (1986): 59–82.

PHYLLIS MAEL

Trifles: The Path to Sisterhood

In 1916 Susan Glaspell wrote *Trifles*, a one-act play to complete the bill at the Wharf Theatre (the other play was *Bound East for Cardiff* by Eugene O'Neill). One commentator on Glaspell's work believes the play was originally intended as a short story, but, according to Glaspell, "the stage took it for its own" (qtd. in Barlow xxi). In 1917, however, Glaspell rewrote the work as a short story, "A Jury of Her Peers," which appeared in *Best Short Stories of 1917*. That work was adapted by Sally Heckel in 1981 for her Academy-Award nominated film.

The setting for all three works is the same: a gloomy farmhouse kitchen belonging to John Wright, recently strangled, and his wife Minnie, now being held in prison for the crime. Three men enter the set: one, the neighboring farmer who discovered the body; another the district attorney; and a third, the sheriff. Two women accompany them: Mrs. Hale, the farmer's wife and childhood friend of Minnie and Mrs. Peters, the sheriff's wife. While the men search the bedroom and barn for clues to a possible motive for the murder, the women move about the kitchen, reconstructing Minnie's dismal life. Through their attentiveness to the "trifles" in her life, the kitchen things considered insignificant by the men, the two women piece together, like patches in a quilt, the events which may have led to the murder. And because they empathize with the missing woman, having lived similar though different lives, they make a moral decision to hide potentially incriminating evidence.

It is unlikely that had either woman been alone, she would have had sufficient understanding or courage to make the vital decision, but as the trifles reveal the arduousness of Minnie's life (and by implication of their own), a web of sisterhood is woven which connects the lives of all three enabling Mrs. Hale and Peters to counter patriarchal law, a decision particularly weighty for Mrs. Peters, who, as she is reminded by the district attorney, is "married to the law" (Glaspell, "Jury" 88).

Having taught both play and short story in my "Images of Women in Literature" classes, I am continually amazed at the power of Glaspell's feminist understanding of the difficult decision with which the two early twentieth century rural women struggle. The volatile discussions which accompany class readings of these works, the questioning of the legality and morality of the women's choices, attest to the relevance of the issues Glaspell raises.

Current feminist research in developmental psychology can help increase our admiration for Glaspell's challenging presentation of the moral dilemma and the way in which Minnie's trifles raise the consciousness of both women, especially Mrs. Peters, moving them from awareness to anger to action. This research can also help us better appreciate Sally Heckel's recent adaptation of these issues to the medium of film, more specifically her use of close-up and composition within the frame, to provide a cinematic equivalent of Glaspell's statements in drama and prose.

Freud would not have been surprised by the decision taken by Mrs. Hale and Peters for in 1925 he wrote that women's superego was never "so inexorable, so impersonal, so independent of its emotional origins as we require it to be in men . . . for women the level of what is ethically normal is different from what it is in men . . . women show less sense of justice than men . . . they are less ready to submit to the great exigencies of life . . . they are more often influenced in their judgment by feelings of affection or hostility" (qtd. in Gilligan, *Voice* 7). Freud's use of value-laden terms such as "less" emerges from a vision of moral development based upon a male model which tends "to regard male behavior as the 'norm' and female behavior as some kind of deviation from that norm" (David McClelland qtd. in Gilligan, *Voice* 14).

Freud's model of mature moral development as "inexorable . . . impersonal . . . independent of emotional origins" reappears in the 1960s as the sixth or post-conventional stage of Lawrence Kohlberg's six stages of moral development. Not surprisingly, when women are given Kohlberg's test, they rarely attain the sixth stage where decisions are based upon universal ethical principles but typically are stuck at the third or fourth (or conventional) levels where decisions are based upon contextual concerns (Gilligan, *Voice* 18).

But Kohlberg's moral scale in turn relies upon a model of human development such as Erik Erikson's "expansion of Freud" (Gilligan, *Voice* 11) where separation, not relationship, becomes the model and measure of growth (Gilligan, "Voice" 509). Freud, Erikson, and Kohlberg, although recognizing that women's development is different from men's, present their model, based upon male experience, as universal.

Recent feminist research in developmental psychology challenges the sexual asymmetry of the patriarchal view in which male development is the norm and women's development is perceived (as with Freud) as "less." Of particular value for a discussion of Glaspell's and Heckel's works are Nancy Chodorow's writings on gender development and Carol Gilligan's on moral development.

According to Chodorow, the "process of becoming a male or female someone in the world begins in infancy with a sense of 'oneness,' a 'primary identification' . . . with the person responsible for early care. Emerging from this phase, every child faces the challenge of separation: distinguishing *self* from *other*. . . . Because women are the primary caretakers of children, that first 'other' is almost without exception female; consequently, boys and girls experience individuation and relationship differently" (qtd in Thurman). For boys, the typical development is more emphatic individuation and firmer ego boundaries, i.e., in order to become male, boys experience more strongly a sense of being "not female." For girls, because the primary parent (or other) is of the same sex, "a basis for 'empathy' [is] built into their primary definition of self" (qtd. in Gilligan, *Voice* 8). They "come to experience themselves as less differentiated than boys, as more continuous with and related to the external object-world. . . . The basic feminine sense of self is connected to the world, the basic masculine sense of self is separate" (Thurman 36).

This distinction in itself carries no value judgment and merely describes a difference. But because theories of psychological development (e.g., Freud's and Erikson's) "focus on individuation . . . and maturity is equated with personal autonomy, concern with relationships appears as a weakness of women rather than as a human strength" (Gilligan, *Voice* 17). If we turn from gender to moral development, a similar pattern emerges. Because women "define themselves in a context of human relationship" (Gilligan, *Voice* 17), their moral decisions differ from those of men. For women, typically, moral problems arise "from conflicting responsibilities rather than from competing rights," require for their "resolution a mode of thinking that is contextual rather than . . . abstract," are concerned more with relationships than rules (Gilligan, *Voice* 19). Since Kohlberg perceives the expansion of moral understanding moving from the preconventional (or individual) through the conventional (or societal) to the post-conventional (or universal), women, who see the self and other as interdependent, whose moral judgments are more closely tied to feelings of empathy and compassion, who see moral problems as problems of responsibility in relationship, are more closely aligned with the conventional, a less mature stage of development (Gilligan, *Voice* 73). Gilligan, however, insists the relational bias in woman's thinking is not a developmental deficiency as traditionally seen by psychologists but a different social and moral understanding. What we have are "two modes of judging, two different constructions of the moral domain—one traditionally associated with masculinity and the public world of social power, the other with femininity and the privacy of domestic interchange" (Gilligan, *Voice* 68).

With this theoretical basis, we can now turn to Glaspell's works and more fully appreciate her astute depiction of these two different modes of judging: the post-conventional revealed through the words and actions of all three men and by Mrs. Peters early in each work, the conventional mode voiced by Mrs. Hale and by Mrs. Peters at the end of each work as her consciousness has been raised through the demeaning remarks made by the men and, more significantly, through her exposure to the trifles of Minnie's life.

From the moment the men enter the kitchen, they begin to judge the absent Minnie according to abstract rules and rights. For example, dirty towels suggest to them that Minnie "was not much of a housekeeper" (18). To Mrs. Hale, however, responding from within a specific context, dirty towels imply that either "there's a great deal of work to be done on a farm" or "towels get dirty awful quick. Men's hands aren't always as clean as they might be" (18–19). As the men continue to criticize or trivialize the domestic sphere (e.g., laughing at the women's concern for broken jars of preserves or their curiosity as to whether Minnie was going to "knot or quilt" her sewing), the stage directions indicate: "the two women move a little closer together" (18).

Their moral "moving closer together" does not occur, however, until Mrs. Peters empathically understands Minnie's situation. For initially, Mrs. Peters parrots the male judgmental mode, demonstrating Glaspell's keen understanding of women's acquiescence to patriarchal law. When Mrs. Hale reproaches the men for disparaging remarks about Minnie's house-keeping, Mrs. Peters timidly responds: "It's no more than their duty" (19). As Mrs. Hale restitches Minnie's erratic sewing on a piece of quilting, Mrs. Peters nervously suggests: "I don't think we ought to touch things" (23). And when Mrs. Hale objects to the men searching and "trying to get Minnie's own house to turn against her," Mrs. Peters replies: "But, Mrs. Hale, the law is the law" (22). Her concern with "duty" and what one "ought to do" support a post-conventional view, corroborating the district attorney's trust in Mrs. Peters as "one of us" (Glaspell, "Jury" 77).

Mrs. Hale, on the contrary, supports Minnie from the outset (although it's not clear that she could or would have taken the final action on her own). She responds to Mrs. Peter's comment that "the law is the law" with "and a bad stove is a bad stove" ("Jury" 80) implying the need to re-interpret abstract law within a particular context. When Mrs. Peters declares: "The law has got to punish crime," Mrs. Hale urges a redefini-tion of one's notion of crime. Reflecting on Minnie's drab and lonely life, she cries: "I wish I'd come over here once in a while! . . . That was crime! Who's going to punish that?" ("Jury" 86).

As Mrs. Peters listens to Mrs. Hale's recollections of Minnie's past and comes into physical contact with Minnie's present, "It was as if something within her, not herself had spoken, and it found in Mrs. Peters something she did not know as herself" ("Jury" 86). Minnie's lonely life evokes mem-ories of the stillness when Mrs. Peter's first baby died while she was homesteading in the Dakotas. Minnie's violent response to the killing of her pet canary recalls murderous feelings in Mrs. Peters when her pet kitten had been brutally slain. Sharing her memories with Mrs. Hale, Mrs. Peters recognizes her connection with other women and, consequently, is capable of moving from a typically male to a more typically female mode of judgment.

In filming the Glaspell works, Sally Heckel utilizes the visual and aural resources of cinema to highlight each trifle, create context, and reinforce relationships. Through close-up (e.g., a jar of preserves, a piece of quilting), the supposedly insignificant kitchen things assume larger-than-life proportions—emphasizing the significance of the domestic sphere. Through a combination of off-screen dialogue and close-up, Heckel creates the context necessary for the women's final decision. For example, when the district attorney is heard to state, "We need a motive," the camera provides a close-up of sugar spilt on a counter (evidence of interrupted work). Another man will state: "We need some definite thing to build a story around," and Heckel offers a close-up of Mrs. Hale's hand on the quilt piece, under which is hidden the dead canary. Thus, while the men speak abstractly off-screen, on-screen, Heckel depicts the particulars, the specific context from which the women will make their moral choice.

A third visual device, composition within the frame, creates relationships, and Heckel will use this to visually unite the women and/or objects. In one frame, she links the remaining jar of preserves, the broken bird cage, and the now-restitched piece of quilt—a visual equivalent of the connections that lead Mrs. Hale and Peters to their joint decision.

Heckel's powerful contemporary film of Glaspell's earlier works attest to the vitality of Glaspell's vision. Fifty years before the current women's movement, Susan Glaspell understood how consciousness raising could empower women to take actions together which they could not take as individuals, how as women share their experiences, they could act out of a new respect for the value of their lives as women, different from, but certainly equal to, the world of men.

WORKS CITED

Barlow, Judith, ed. Plays by American Women. New York: Avon, 1981.

Gilligan, Carol. "In a Different Voice: Women's Conceptions of Self and Morality." Harvard Educational Review 47 (1977): 509.

———. In a Different Voice. Cambridge: Harvard UP, 1982.

Glaspell, Susan. "A Jury of Her Peers." The Wadsworth Casebook Series for Reading, Research, and Writing: Trifles. Ed. Donna Winchell. Boston: Wadsworth, 2004. 70–88.

———. Trifles. The Wadsworth Casebook Series for Reading, Research, and Writing: Trifles. Ed. Donna Winchell. Boston: Wadsworth, 2004. 15–28.

Thurman, Judith. "The Basics: Chodorow's Theory of Gender." Ms. Sept. 1982: 35–36.

KAREN F. STEIN

The Women's World of Glaspell's *Trifles*

Susan Glaspell's murder mystery, *Trifles*, explores sympathetically the lives of middle-aged, married, rural women, characters who would usually be minor figures in a play. In this way, *Trifles* (published in 1920) is a uniquely female and, indeed, feminist document.

Two farm women gather some personal belongings for Minnie Wright, jailed on suspicion of her husband John's murder. Observing the details of daily life in the bleak Wright household, Mrs. Peters and Mrs. Hale deduce the events which led Mrs. Wright to hang her tyrannical husband. The lack of a telephone, the shabby furniture, the much-mended clothing, and a canary with a broken neck bear mute but telling witness to the harsh meanness and cruelty of John Wright. Considering Minnie her husband's victim (like her symbolic analogue, the strangled songbird), the women conspire to hide the evidence they discover.

Trifles is an anomaly in the murder mystery genre, which is predominantly a masculine tour de force. We are used to seeing the detective as an active hero, proving his skill and ruthlessness in a brilliant intellectual game. In the classic sleuth story, the detective is hired by a desperate victim, frequently a woman, to solve a problem through his expertise. The hero may incur risks in his investigation, but his willingness to do so is further proof of his courage and power. In solving the mystery, the detective demonstrates his shrewdness and acuity. His successful investigation is the piecing together of a difficult puzzle; his reward for success is a handsome fee, the admiration of all who have observed him, and frequently, the love of the woman who hired him. But he remains intriguingly aloof, uncommitted.

The scenario of *Trifles*, however, is quite different. Here, the detectives are the very women that the powerful police, sheriffs, and detectives see as trivial, even ludicrous. Two middle-aged married women, lacking all glamour, they unravel the mystery from positions of weakness, not strength. Furthermore, as we will see, they utilize their intrinsic "femaleness," their triviality in the eyes of men, their concern with the minutiae of women's lives, to solve the mystery. What is most unusual, however, is that they do not remain objective observers; they become personally involved, and, through their successful investigations they gain human sympathy and valuable insights into their own lives. This growth, rather than the sleuthing process, is the play's focal point.

The woman themselves are "trifles" to the busy, efficient men who leave them behind to tidy up while they (the men) investigate the murder of John Wright, searching upstairs in the bedroom for clues to the motive. The county attorney, intent on finding physical evidence, fails to pursue two references to Wright's meanness. But, as the women attend to the trifling details of packing clothes and cleaning up the kitchen, they observe carefully and come to understand the mystery of the missing motive. The clues are a strangled canary and the irregular stitching, indicative of tension, in a piece of patchwork Mrs. Wright was sewing. Thus, while the men search for—and fail to find—external signs such as forced entry into the house, their wives interpret the emotional significance of small details, learning of the narrowness of Minnie's life, her frustration, and her anger.

Interpreted similarly in its social and psychological contexts, the patchwork process becomes an objective correlative for the lives of these New England matrons. The patchwork quilt, composed of remnant fabric scraps and salvaged bits of old garments, is a uniquely American solution to the dilemma of keeping warm in an economy of scarcity before the introduction of central heating. Patchwork is a task demanding patient and painstaking attention to repetitive, minute details: a quilt may contain as many as 30,000 pieces, each one-half inch by three-quarters of an inch in size (Hedges).[1] To women, in their homemaking role, went the task of hoarding the fabric scraps and stitching them into quilts. Girls were set to sewing samplers and quilt squares as soon as they were old enough to hold needles; they were expected to busy themselves with needlework whenever they had no more urgent chores. Through this apprenticeship, girls were trained in the docility and discipline which society valued in its women. At the same time, the apprenticeship in quilting and other household tasks in a society with sharp gender-role differentiation bound women of a household together. Networks of female friendship and mutual assistance were central in the lives of eighteenth- and nineteenth-century women (Smith-Rosenberg).

Quilts were made primarily for their utility, but they also offered an outlet for creativity that often had no other available channel of expression. For the many women who had no knowledge of reading and writing, and who could not have spent their time in such nonproductive activities, patchwork became a means of artistic self-expression. In the quilt patterns and the names for them that their makers devised, women told the stories of their lives. Such names as "Baby's Blocks," "Log Cabin," "Corn and Beans," "Covered Wagon Trail," "Underground Railroad," and "Union

Star" give us an insight into the daily routines and political sentiment of their creators.

The patchwork squares were pieced together in soltude, often in between and after the completion of the round of chores which was women's lot. The quilting itself, however, the joining of the patterned patchwork upper layer to the lining and the backing, was done in a communal setting, the quilting bee. Groups of women, friends and skilled seamstresses, would gather around the quilting frame to cooperate in the tedious task of quilting. The quilting bee was one of the main social events for women whose daily lives kept them isolated from each other. For many years, we have thought of the quilting bee as an occasion for idle gossip. But, we are gradually learning to understand and appreciate the importance of these parties as vehicles for sharing knowledge and camaraderie, for developing and strengthening social support groups, and for accomplishing a difficult job effectively.

Quiltmaking brought neighbors and friends together in a holiday spirit to cooperate in the production of useful and beautiful artifacts. In *Trifles*, as Mrs. Wright's neighbors view the separate fragments of the incomplete quilt, the mood is not festive but funereal. They have come not to join in the warm and social act of creation, but to clean up the debris of destruction. Through the sympathetic eyes of her neighbors, we are made to see the frustration of all Mrs. Wright's hopes for beauty, order, and happiness.

Observing the bits of evidence, a strangled bird which John Wright must have killed, the tight stitching which was the woman's reined-in response to this act of wanton cruelty, the women become poignantly aware of the emotional poverty of their neighbor's life. We feel with them her thwarted needs for song and companionship. Mrs. Hale reflects, "Wright wouldn't like the bird—a thing that sang. She used to sing. He killed that, too." Through the women's identification with her, we understand Minnie's desperate loneliness which drove her to do away with her brutal husband.

MRS HALE

If there'd been years and years of nothing, then a bird to sing to you, it would be awful—still, after the bird was. Still.

MRS. PETERS

I know what stillness is. When we homesteaded in Dakota, and my first baby died—after he was two years old, and me with no other then—

Out of their sympathy for Mrs. Wright as a woman they perceive to be more sinned against than sinning, the neighbors conceal their discovery of the motive from the male investigators. After ripping out the uneven stitches and removing the strangled canary, they respond with terse irony to the county attorney's patronizing question about Mrs. Wright's quilting, "We call it—knot it, Mr. Henderson."

In their decision to conceal the evidence, the women in *Trifles* affirm their ties of loyalty and affection to other women. Mrs. Hale laments her guilt in letting this communality lapse: "Oh, I *wish* I'd come here once in a while! That was a crime! That was a crime! Who's going to punish that?" The need for cooperation is manifested throughout the play, in the references to shared tasks such as quiltmaking, and in their remarks about their own needs for companionship. In fact, the discovery and interpretation of the clues and the suppression of the findings is a shared process, diametrically opposite to the solo virtuosity usually displayed by male detectives. Further emphasis on the mutual understanding and aid women offer each other was inherent in Glaspell's title for the short story from which she derived this play, "A Jury of Her Peers." The women here realize, through their involvement in the murder investigation, that only by joining together can they, isolated and insignificant in their society, obtain for themselves and extend to others the support and sympathy that will help them endure the loneliness and unceasing labor required of them. For these women, solving the murder is not a disinterested act, but a cooperative endeavor which leads them to a knowledge essential for their survival as females in a hostile or indifferent world.

NOTES

1. For an art critic's assessment of the esthetics of women's quilts, see Patricia Mainardi, "Quilts: The Great American Art." *Radical America* 7.1 (1973): 36–68.

WORKS CITED

Hedges, Elaine. "Quilts and Women's Culture." The Radical Teacher 4 (March 1977).

Smith-Rosenberg, Caroll. "The Female World of Love and Ritual: Relations Between Women in Nineteenth Century America." Signs: Journal of Women in Culture and Society 1.1 (1973): 1–29.

SUSAN GLASPELL

A Jury of Her Peers

When Martha Hale opened the storm door and got a cut of the north wind, she ran back for her big woolen scarf. As she hurriedly wound that round her head her eye made a scandalized sweep of her kitchen. It was no ordinary thing that called her away—it was probably farther from ordinary than anything that had ever happened in Dickson County. But what her eye took in was that her kitchen was in no shape for leaving: her bread all ready for mixing, half the flour sifted and half unsifted.

She hated to see things half done; but she had been at that when the team from town stopped to get Mr. Hale, and then the sheriff came running in to say his wife wished Mrs. Hale would come too—adding, with a grin, that he guessed she was getting scarey and wanted another woman along. So she had dropped everything right where it was.

"Martha!" now came her husband's impatient voice. "Don't keep folks waiting out here in the cold."

She again opened the storm door, and this time joined the three men and the one woman waiting for her in the big two-seated buggy.

After she had the robes tucked around her she took another look at the woman who sat beside her on the back seat. She had met Mrs. Peters the year before at the county fair, and the thing she remembered about her was that she didn't seem like a sheriff's wife. She was small and thin and didn't have a strong voice. Mrs. Gorman, sheriff's wife before Gorman went out and Peters came in, had a voice that somehow seemed to be backing up the law with every word. But if Mrs. Peters didn't look like a sheriff's wife, Peters made it up in looking like a sheriff. He was to a dot the kind of man who could get himself elected sheriff—a heavy man with a big voice, who was particularly genial with the law-abiding, as if to make it plain that he knew the difference between criminals and non-criminals. And right there it came to Mrs. Hale's mind, with a stab, that this man who was so pleasant and lively with all of them was going to the Wrights' now as a sheriff.

"The country's not very pleasant this time of year," Mrs. Peters at last ventured, as if she felt they ought to be talking as well as the men.

Mrs. Hale scarcely finished her reply, for they had gone up a little hill and could see the Wright place now, and seeing it did not make her feel like talking. It looked very lonesome this cold March morning. It had always been a lonesome-looking place. It was down in a hollow, and the poplar trees around it were lonesome-looking trees. The men were looking at it and talking about what had happened. The county attorney was bending to one side of the buggy, and kept looking steadily at the place as they drew up to it.

"I'm glad you came with me," Mrs. Peters said nervously, as the two women were about to follow the men in through the kitchen door.

Even after she had her foot on the doorstep, her hand on the knob, Martha Hale had a moment of feeling she could not cross the threshold. And the reason it seemed she couldn't cross it now was simply because she hadn't crossed it before. Time and time again it had been in her mind, "I ought to go over and see Minnie Foster"—she still thought of her as Minnie Foster, though for twenty years she had been Mrs. Wright. And then there was always something to do and Minnie Foster would go from her mind. But *now* she could come.

The men went over to the stove. The women stood close together by the 10 door. Young Henderson, the county attorney, turned around and said, "Come up to the fire, ladies."

Mrs. Peters took a step forward, then stopped. "I'm not—cold," she said.

And so the two women stood by the door, at first not even so much as looking around the kitchen.

The men talked for a minute about what a good thing it was the sheriff sent his deputy out that morning to make a fire for them, and then Sheriff Peters stepped back from the stove, unbuttoned his outer coat, and leaned his hands on the kitchen table in a way that seemed to mark the beginning of official business. "Now, Mr. Hale," he said in a sort of semiofficial voice, "before we move things about, you tell Mr. Henderson just what it was you saw when you came here yesterday morning."

The county attorney was looking around the kitchen.

"By the way," he said, "has anything been moved?" He turned to the 15 sheriff. "Are things just as you left them yesterday?"

Peters looked from cupboard to sink; from that to a small worn rocker a little to one side of the kitchen table.

"It's just the same."

"Somebody should have been left here yesterday," said the county attorney.

"Oh—yesterday," returned the sheriff, with a little gesture as of yesterday having been more than he could bear to think of. "When I had to send Frank to Morris Center for that man who went crazy—let me tell you, I had my hands full *yesterday*. I knew you could get back from

Omaha by today, George, and as long as I went over everything here myself—

"Well, Mr. Hale," said the county attorney, in a way of letting what was   20 past and gone go, "tell just what happened when you came here yesterday morning."

Mrs. Hale, still leaning against the door, had that sinking feeling of the mother whose child is about to speak a piece. Lewis often wandered along and got things mixed up in a story. She hoped that he would tell this straight and plain, and not say unnecessary things that would just make things harder for Minnie Foster. He didn't begin at once, and she noticed that he looked queer—as if standing in that kitchen and having to tell what he had seen there yesterday morning made him almost sick.

"Yes, Mr. Hale?" the county attorney reminded.

"Harry and I had started to town with a load of potatoes," Mrs. Hale's husband began.

Harry was Mrs. Hale's oldest boy. He wasn't with them now, for the very good reason that those potatoes never got to town yesterday and he was taking them this morning, so he hadn't been home when the sheriff stopped to say he wanted Mr. Hale to come over to the Wright place and tell the county attorney his story there, where he could point it all out. With all Mrs. Hale's other emotions came the fear that maybe Harry wasn't dressed warm enough—they hadn't any of them realized how that north wind did bite.

"We come along this road," Hale was going on, with a motion of his hand   25 to the road over which they had just come, "and as we got in sight of the house I says to Harry, 'I'm goin' to see if I can't get John Wright to take a telephone.' You see," he explained to Henderson, "unless I can get somebody to go in with me they won't come out this branch road except for a price *I* can't pay. I'd spoke to Wright about it once before; but he put me off, saying folks talked too much anyway, and all he asked was peace and quiet—guess you know about how much he talked himself. But I thought maybe if I went to the house and talked about it before his wife, and said all the women-folks liked the telephones, and that in this lonesome stretch of road it would be a good thing—well, I said to Harry that that was what I was going to say—though I said at the same time that I didn't know as what his wife wanted made much difference to John—"

Now, there he was!—saying things he didn't need to say. Mrs. Hale tried to catch her husband's eye, but fortunately the county attorney interrupted with:

"Let's talk about that a little later, Mr. Hale. I do want to talk about that, but I'm anxious now to get along to just what happened when you got here."

When he began this time, it was very deliberately and carefully: "I didn't see or hear anything. I knocked at the door. And still it was all quiet inside. I knew they must be up—it was past eight o'clock. So I knocked again, louder, and I thought I heard somebody say 'Come in.' I wasn't sure—I'm not sure yet. But I opened the door—this door," jerking a hand toward the door by which the two women stood, "and there, in that rocker"—pointing to it—"sat Mrs. Wright."

Every one in the kitchen looked at the rocker. It came into Mrs. Hale's   30 mind that that rocker didn't look in the least like Minnie Foster—the Minnie Foster of twenty years before. It was a dingy red, with wooden rungs up the back, and the middle rung was gone, and the chair sagged to one side.

"How did she—look?" the county attorney was inquiring.

"Well," said Hale, "she looked—queer."

"How do you mean—queer?"

As he asked it he took out a notebook and pencil. Mrs. Hale did not like the sight of that pencil. She kept her eye fixed on her husband, as if to keep him from saying unnecessary things that would go into that notebook and make trouble.

Hale did speak guardedly, as if the pencil had affected him too.   35

"Well, as if she didn't know what she was going to do next. And kind of—done up."

"How did she seem to feel about your coming?"

"Why, I don't think she minded—one way or other. She didn't pay much attention. I said, 'Ho' do, Mrs. Wright? It's cold, ain't it?' And she said, 'Is it?'—and went on pleatin' at her apron.

"Well, I was surprised. She didn't ask me to come up to the stove, or to sit down, but just set there, not even lookin' at me. And so I said: 'I want to see John.'

"And then she—laughed. I guess you would call it a laugh.   40

"I thought of Harry and the team outside, so I said, a little sharp, 'Can I see John?' 'No,' says she—kind of dull like. 'Ain't he home?' says I. Then she looked at me. 'Yes,' says she, 'he's home.' 'Then why can't I see him?' I asked her, out of patience with her now. ''Cause he's dead,' says she, just as quiet and dull—and fell to pleatin' her apron. 'Dead?' says I, like you do when you can't take in what you've heard.

"She just nodded her head, not getting a bit excited, but rockin' back and forth.

" 'Why—where is he?' says I, not knowing *what* to say.

"She just pointed upstairs—like this"—pointing to the room above.

"I got up, with the idea of going up there myself. By this time I—didn't know what to do. I walked from there to here; then I says: 'Why, what did he die of?'   45

" 'He died of a rope around his neck,' says she; and just went on pleatin' at her apron."

Hale stopped speaking, and stood staring at the rocker, as if he were still seeing the woman who had sat there the morning before. Nobody spoke; it was as if every one were seeing the woman who had sat there the morning before.

"And what did you do then?" the county attorney at last broke the silence.

"I went out and called Harry. I thought I might—need help. I got Harry in, and we went upstairs." His voice fell almost to a whisper. "There he was—lying over the—"

"I think I'd rather have you go into that upstairs," the county attorney interrupted, "where you can point it all out. Just go on now with the rest of the story."   50

"Well, my first thought was to get that rope off. It looked—"

He stopped, his face twitching.

"But Harry, he went up to him, and he said, 'No, he's dead all right, and we'd better not touch anything.' So we went downstairs.

"She was still sitting that same way. 'Has anybody been notified?' I asked. 'No,' says she, unconcerned."

" 'Who did this, Mrs. Wright?' said Harry. He said it businesslike, and she stopped pleatin' at her apron. 'I don't know,' she says. 'You don't *know?*' says Harry. 'Weren't you sleepin' in the bed with him?' 'Yes,' says she, 'but I was on the inside.' 'Somebody slipped a rope round his neck and strangled him, and you didn't wake up?' says Harry. 'I didn't wake up,' she said after him.   55

"We may have looked as if we didn't see how that could be, for after a minute she said, 'I sleep sound.'

"Harry was going to ask her more questions, but I said maybe that weren't our business; maybe we ought to let her tell her story first to the coroner or the sheriff. So Harry went fast as he could over to High Road—the Rivers's place, where there's a telephone."

"And what did she do when she knew you had gone for the coroner?" The attorney got his pencil in his hand all ready for writing.

"She moved from that chair to this one over here"—Hale pointed to a small chair in the corner—"and just sat there with her hands held together and looking down. I got a feeling that I ought to make some conversation, so I said I had come in to see if John wanted to put in a telephone; and at that she started to laugh, and then she stopped and looked at me—scared."

At the sound of the moving pencil the man who was telling the story 60 looked up.

"I dunno—maybe it wasn't scared," he hastened; "I wouldn't like to say it was. Soon Harry got back, and then Dr. Lloyd came, and you, Mr. Peters, and so I guess that's all I know that you don't."

He said that last with relief, and moved a little, as if relaxing. Every one moved a little. The county attorney walked toward the stair door.

"I guess we'll go upstairs first—then out to the barn and around there." He paused and looked around the kitchen.

"You're convinced there was nothing important here?" he asked the 65 sheriff. "Nothing that would—point to any motive?"

The sheriff too looked all around, as if to re-convince himself.

"Nothing here but kitchen things," he said, with a little laugh for the insignificance of kitchen things.

The county attorney was looking at the cupboard—a peculiar, ungainly structure, half closet and half cupboard, the upper part of it being built in the wall, and the lower part just the old-fashioned kitchen cupboard. As if its queerness attracted him, he got a chair and opened the upper part and looked in. After a moment he drew his hand away sticky.

"Here's a nice mess," he said resentfully.

The two women had drawn nearer, and now the sheriff's wife spoke. 70

"Oh—her fruit," she said, looking to Mrs. Hale for sympathetic understanding. She turned back to the county attorney and explained. "She worried about that when it turned so cold last night. She said the fire would go out and her jars might burst."

Mrs. Peters's husband broke into a laugh.

"Well, can you beat the women! Held for murder, and worrying about her preserves!"

The young attorney set his lips.

"I guess before we're through with her she may have something more 75 serious than preserves to worry about."

"Oh, well," said Mrs. Hale's husband, with good-natured superiority, "women are used to worrying over trifles."

The two women moved a little closer together. Neither of them spoke. The county attorney seemed suddenly to remember his manners—and think of his future.

"And yet," said he, with the gallantry of a young politician, "for all their worries, what would we do without the ladies?"

The women did not speak, did not unbend. He went to the sink and began washing his hands. He turned to wipe them on the roller wheel— whirled it for a cleaner place.

"Dirty towels! Not much of a housekeeper, would you say, ladies?"   80

He kicked his foot against some dirty pans under the sink.

"There's a great deal of work to be done on a farm," said Mrs. Hale stiffly.

"To be sure. And yet"—with a little bow to her—"I know there are some Dickson County farmhouses that do not have such roller towels." He gave it a pull to expose its full length again.

"Those towels get dirty awful quick. Men's hands aren't always as clean as they might be."

"Ah, loyal to your sex, I see," he laughed. He stopped and gave her a   85 keen look. "But you and Mrs. Wright were neighbors. I suppose you were friends, too."

Martha Hale shook her head.

"I've seen little enough of her of late years. I've not been in this house— it's more than a year."

"And why was that? You didn't like her?"

"I liked her well enough," she replied with spirit. "Farmer's wives have their hands full, Mr. Henderson. And then—" She looked around the kitchen.

"Yes?" he encouraged.   90

"It never seemed a very cheerful place," said she, more to herself than to him.

"No," he agreed; "I don't think any one would call it cheerful. I shouldn't say she had the homemaking instinct."

"Well, I don't know as Wright had, either," she muttered.

"You mean they didn't get on very well?" he was very quick to ask.

"No; I don't mean anything," she answered, with decision. As she   95 turned a little away from him, she added: "But I don't think a place would be any the cheerfuler for John Wright's bein' in it."

"I'd like to talk to you about that a little later, Mrs. Hale," he said. "I'm anxious to get the lay of things upstairs now."

He moved toward the stair door, followed by the two men.

"I suppose anything Mrs. Peters does'll be all right?" the sheriff inquired. "She was supposed to take in some clothes for her, you know— and a few little things. We left in such a hurry yesterday."

The county attorney looked at the two women whom they were leaving alone among the kitchen things.

"Yes—Mrs. Peters," he said, his glance resting on the woman who was **100** not Mrs. Peters, the big farmer woman who stood behind the sheriff's wife. "Of course Mrs. Peters is one of us," he said, in a manner of entrusting responsibility. "And keep your eye out, Mrs. Peters, for anything that might be of use. No telling; you women might come upon a clue to the motive—and that's the thing we need."

Mr. Hale rubbed his face after the fashion of a show man getting ready for a pleasantry.

"But would the women know a clue if they did come upon it?" he said; and, having delivered himself of this, he followed the others through the stair door.

The women stood motionless and silent, listening to the footsteps, first upon the stairs, then in the room above them.

Then, as if releasing herself from something strange, Mrs. Hale began to arrange the dirty pans under the sink, which the county attorney's disdainful push of the foot had deranged.

"I'd hate to have men comin' into my kitchen," she said testily— **105** "snoopin' round and criticizin'."

"Of course it's no more than their duty," said the sheriff's wife, in her manner of timid acquiescence.

"Duty's all right," replied Mrs. Hale bluffly; "but I guess that deputy sheriff that come out to make the fire might have got a little of this on." She gave the roller towel a pull. "Wish I'd thought of that sooner! Seems mean to talk about her for not having things slicked up, when she had to come away in such a hurry."

She looked around the kitchen. Certainly it was not "slicked up." Her eye was held by a bucket of sugar on a low shelf. The cover was off the wooden bucket, and beside it was a paper bag—half full.

Mrs. Hale moved toward it.

"She was putting this in here," she said to herself—slowly. **110**

She thought of the flour in her kitchen at home—half sifted, half not sifted. She had been interrupted, and had left things half done. What had interrupted Minnie Foster? Why had that work been left half done? She made a move as if to finish it,—unfinished things always bothered

her,—and then she glanced around and saw that Mrs. Peters was watch-
ing her—and she didn't want Mrs. Peters to get that feeling she had got
of work begun and then—for some reason—not finished.

"It's a shame about her fruit," she said, and walked toward the cupboard that the county attorney had opened, and got on the chair, mur-
muring: "I wonder if it's all gone."

It was a sorry enough looking sight, but "Here's one that's all right,"
she said at last. She held it toward the light. "This is cherries, too." She
looked again. "I declare I believe that's the only one."

With a sigh, she got down from the chair, went to the sink, and wiped
off the bottle.

"She'll feel awful bad, after all her hard work in the hot weather. I 115
remember the afternoon I put up my cherries last summer."

She set the bottle on the table, and, with another sigh, started to sit
down in the rocker. But she did not sit down. Something kept her from
sitting down in that chair. She straightened—stepped back, and half
turned away, stood looking at it, seeing the woman who sat there "pleatin'
at her apron."

The thin voice of the sheriff's wife broke in upon her: "I must be getting those things from the front room closet." She opened the door into the
other room, started in, stepped back. "You coming with me, Mrs. Hale?"
she asked nervously. "You—you could help me get them."

They were soon back—the stark coldness of that shut-up room was not
a thing to linger in.

"My!" said Mrs. Peters, dropping the things on the table and hurrying
to the stove.

Mrs. Hale stood examining the clothes the woman who was being 120
detained in town had said she wanted.

"Wright was close!" she exclaimed, holding up a shabby black skirt that
bore the marks of much making over. "I think maybe that's why she kept
so much to herself. I s'pose she felt she couldn't do her part; and then, you
don't enjoy things when you feel shabby. She used to wear pretty clothes
and be lively—when she was Minnie Foster, one of the town girls, singing
in the choir. But that—oh, that was twenty years ago."

With a carefulness in which there was something tender, she folded
the shabby clothes and piled them at one corner of the table. She looked
at Mrs. Peters, and there was something in the other woman's look that
irritated her.

"She don't care," she said to herself. "Much difference it makes to her
whether Minnie Foster had pretty clothes when she was a girl."

Then she looked again, and she wasn't so sure; in fact, she hadn't at any time been perfectly sure about Mrs. Peters. She had that shrinking manner, and yet her eyes looked as if they could see a long way into things.

"This all you was to take in?" asked Mrs. Hale.   125

"No," said the sheriff's wife; "she said she wanted an apron. Funny thing to want," she ventured in her nervous little way, "for there's not much to get you dirty in jail, goodness knows. But I suppose just to make her feel more natural. If you're used to wearing an apron—. She said they were in the bottom drawer of this cupboard. Yes—here they are. And then her little shawl that always hung on the stair door."

She took the small gray shawl from behind the door leading upstairs, and stood a minute looking at it.

Suddenly Mrs. Hale took a quick step toward the other woman.

"Mrs. Peters!"

"Yes, Mrs. Hale?"   130

"Do you think she—did it?"

A frightened look blurred the other things in Mrs. Peter's eyes.

"Oh, I don't know," she said, in a voice that seemed to shrink away from the subject.

"Well, I don't think she did," affirmed Mrs. Hale stoutly. "Asking for an apron, and her little shawl. Worryin' about her fruit."

"Mr. Peters says—." Footsteps were heard in the room above; she 135 stopped, looked up, then went on in a lowered voice: "Mr. Peters says—it looks bad for her. Mr. Henderson is awful sarcastic in a speech, and he's going to make fun of her saying she didn't—wake up."

For a moment Mrs. Hale had no answer. Then, "Well, I guess John Wright didn't wake up—when they was slippin' that rope under his neck," she muttered.

"No, it's *strange*," breathed Mrs. Peters. "They think it was such a— funny way to kill a man."

She began to laugh; at the sound of the laugh, abruptly stopped.

"That's just what Mr. Hale said," said Mrs. Hale, in a resolutely nat- ural voice. "There was a gun in the house. He says that's what he can't understand."

"Mr. Henderson said, coming out, that what was needed for the case 140 was a motive. Something to show anger—or sudden feeling."

"Well, I don't see any signs of anger around here," said Mrs. Hale. "I don't—"

She stopped. It was as if her mind tripped on something. Her eye was caught by a dish-towel in the middle of the kitchen table. Slowly she moved toward the table. One half of it was wiped clean, the other half messy. Her eyes made a slow, almost unwilling turn to the bucket of sugar and the half empty bag beside it. Things begun—and not finished.

After a moment she stepped back, and said, in that manner of releasing herself:

"Wonder how they're finding things upstairs? I hope she had it a little more red up up there. You know,"—she paused, and feeling gathered,—"it seems kind of *sneaking*; locking her up in town and coming out here to get her own house to turn against her!"

"But, Mrs. Hale," said the sheriff's wife, "the law is the law."   145

"I s'pose 'tis," answered Mrs. Hale shortly.

She turned to the stove, saying something about that fire not being much to brag of. She worked with it a minute, and when she straightened up she said aggressively:

"The law is the law—and a bad stove is a bad stove. How'd you like to cook on this?"—pointing with a poker to the broken lining. She opened the oven door and started to express her opinion of the oven; but she was swept into her own thoughts, thinking of what it would mean, year after year, to have that stove to wrestle with. The thought of Minnie Foster trying to bake in that oven—and the thought of her never going over to see Minnie Foster—.

She was startled by hearing Mrs. Peters say: "A person gets discouraged—and loses heart."

The sheriff's wife had looked from the stove to the sink—to the pail of 150 water which had been carried in from outside. The two women stood there silent, above them the footsteps of the men who were looking for evidence against the woman who had worked in that kitchen. That look of seeing into things, of seeing through a thing to something else, was in the eyes of the sheriff's wife now. When Mrs. Hale next spoke to her, it was gently:

"Better loosen up your things, Mrs. Peters. We'll not feel them when we go out."

Mrs. Peters went to the back of the room to hang up the fur tippet she was wearing. A moment later she exclaimed, "Why, she was piecing a quilt," and held up a large sewing basket piled high with quilt pieces.

Mrs. Hale spread some of the blocks on the table.

"It's log-cabin pattern," she said, putting several of them together. "Pretty, isn't it?"

They were so engaged with the quilt that they did not hear the foot- 155 steps on the stairs. Just as the stair door opened Mrs. Hale was saying:

"Do you suppose she was going to quilt it or just knot it?"

The sheriff threw up his hands.

"They wonder whether she was going to quilt it or just knot it!"

There was a laugh for the ways of women, a warming of hands over the stove, and then the county attorney said briskly:

"Well, let's go right out to the barn and get that cleared up."   160

"I don't see as there's anything so strange," Mrs. Hale said resentfully, after the outside door had closed on the three men—"our taking up our time with little things while we're waiting for them to get the evidence. I don't see as it's anything to laugh about."

"Of course they've got awful important things on their minds," said the sheriff's wife apologetically.

They returned to the inspection of the blocks for the quilt. Mrs. Hale was looking at the fine, even sewing, and preoccupied with thoughts of the woman who had done that sewing, when she heard the sheriff's wife say, in a queer tone:

"Why, look at this one."

She turned to take the block held out to her.   165

"The sewing," said Mrs. Peters, in a troubled way. "All the rest of them have been so nice and even—but—this one. Why, it looks as if she didn't know what she was about!"

Their eyes met—something flashed to life, passed between them; then, as if with an effort, they seemed to pull away from each other. A moment Mrs. Hale sat there, her hands folded over that sewing which was so unlike all the rest of the sewing. Then she had pulled a knot and drawn the threads.

"Oh, what are you doing, Mrs. Hale?" asked the sheriff's wife, startled.

"Just pulling out a stitch or two that's not sewed very good." said Mrs. Hale mildly.

"I don't think we ought to touch things," Mrs. Peters said, a little 170 helplessly.

"I'll just finish up this end," answered Mrs. Hale, still in that mild, matter-of-fact faction.

She threaded a needle and started to replace bad sewing with good. For a little while she sewed in silence. Then, in that thin, timid voice, she heard:

"Mrs. Hale!"

"Yes, Mrs. Peters?"

"What do you suppose she was so—nervous about?"   175

"Oh, *I* don't know," said Mrs. Hale, as if dismissing a thing not important enough to spend much time on. "I don't know as she was—nervous.
I sew awful queer sometimes when I'm just tired."

She cut a thread, and out of the corner of her eye looked up at Mrs.
Peters. The small, lean face of the sheriff's wife seemed to have tightened
up. Her eyes had that look of peering into something. But the next
moment she moved, and said in her thin, indecisive way:

"Well, I must get those clothes wrapped. They may be through sooner
than we think. I wonder where I could find a piece of paper—and string."

"In that cupboard, maybe," suggested Mrs. Hale, after a glance around.

One piece of the crazy sewing remained unripped. Mrs. Peters's back 180
turned, Martha Hale now scrutinized that piece, compared it with the
dainty, accurate sewing of the other blocks. The difference was startling.
Holding this block made her feel queer, as if the distracted thoughts of the
woman who had perhaps turned to it to try and quiet herself were com-
municating themselves to her.

Mrs. Peter's voice roused her.

"Here's a birdcage," she said. "Did she have a bird, Mrs. Hale?"

"Why, I don't know whether she did or not." She turned to look at the
cage Mrs. Peters was holding up. "I've not been here in so long." She
sighed. "There was a man around last year selling canaries cheap—but I
don't know as she took one. Maybe she did. She used to sing real pretty
herself."

Mrs. Peters looked around the kitchen.

"Seems kind of funny to think of a bird here." She half laughed—an 185
attempt to put up a barrier. "But she must have had one—or why would
she have a cage? I wonder what happened to it?"

"I suppose maybe the cat got it," suggested Mrs. Hale, resuming her
sewing.

"No, she didn't have a cat. She's got that feeling some people have about
cats—being afraid of them. When they brought her to our house yesterday, my cat got in the room, and she was real upset and asked me to take
it out."

"My sister Bessie was like that," laughed Mrs. Hale.

The sheriff's wife did not reply. The silence made Mrs. Hale turn
around. Mrs. Peters was examining the birdcage.

"Look at this door," she said slowly. "It's broke. One hinge has been 190
pulled apart."

Mrs. Hale came nearer.

"Looks as if some one must have been—rough with it."

Again their eyes met—startled, questioning, apprehensive. For a moment neither spoke nor stirred. Then Mrs. Hale, turning away, said brusquely:

"If they're going to find any evidence, I wish they'd be about it. I don't like this place.

"But I'm awful glad you came with me, Mrs. Hale." Mrs. Peters put the 195 birdcage on the table and sat down. "It would be lonesome for me—sitting here alone.

"Yes, it would, wouldn't it?" agreed Mrs. Hale, a certain determined naturalness in her voice. She picked up the sewing, but now it dropped in her lap, and she murmured in a different voice: "But I tell you what I *do* wish, Mrs. Peters. I wish I had come over sometimes when she was here. I wish—I had."

"But of course you were awful busy, Mrs. Hale. Your house—and your children."

"I could've come," retorted Mrs. Hale shortly. "I stayed away because it weren't cheerful—and that's why I ought to have come. I"—she looked around—"I've never liked this place. Maybe because it's down in a hollow and you don't see the road. I don't know what it is, but it's a lonesome place, and always was. I wish I had come over to see Minnie Foster sometimes. I can see now—" She did not put it into words.

"Well, you mustn't reproach yourself," counseled Mrs. Peters. "Somehow, we just don't see how it is with other folks till—something comes up."

"Not having children makes less work," mused Mrs. Hale, after a 200 silence, "but it makes a quiet house—and Wright out to work all day— and no company when he did come in. Did you know John Wright, Mrs. Peters?"

"Not to know him. I've seen him in town. They say he was a good man."

"Yes—good," conceded John Wright's neighbor grimly. "He didn't drink, and kept his word as well as most, I guess, and paid his debts. But he was a hard man, Mrs. Peters. Just to pass the time of day with him—." She stopped, shivered a little. "Like a raw wind that gets to the bone." Her eye fell upon the cage on the table before her, and she added, almost bitterly: "I should think she would've wanted a bird!"

Suddenly she leaned forward, looking intently at the cage. "But what do you s'pose went wrong with it?"

"I don't know," returned Mrs. Peters; "unless it got sick and died."

But after she said it she reached over and swung the broken door. 205 Both women watched it as if somehow held by it.

"You didn't know—her?" Mrs. Hale asked, a gentler note in her voice.

"Not till they brought her yesterday," said the sheriff's wife.

"She—come to think of it, she was kind of like a bird herself. Real sweet and pretty, but kind of timid and—fluttery. How—she—did—change."

That held her for a long time. Finally, as if struck with a happy thought and relieved to get back to everyday things, she exclaimed:

"Tell you what, Mrs. Peters, why don't you take the quilt in with you? 210 It might take up her mind."

"Why, I think that's a real nice idea, Mrs. Hale," agreed the sheriff's wife, as if she too were glad to come into the atmosphere of a simple kindness. "There couldn't possibly be any objection to that, could there? Now, just what will I take? I wonder if her patches are here—and her things."

They turned to the sewing basket.

"Here's some red," said Mrs. Hale, bringing out a roll of cloth. Underneath that was a box. "Here, maybe her scissors are in here—and her things." She held it up. "What a pretty box! I'll warrant that was something she had a long time ago—when she was a girl."

She held it in her hand a moment; then, with a little sigh, opened it.

Instantly her hand went to her nose. 215

"Why—!"

Mrs. Peters drew nearer—then turned away.

"There's something wrapped up in this piece of silk," faltered Mrs. Hale.

"This isn't her scissors," said Mrs. Peters in a shrinking voice.

Her hand not steady, Mrs. Hale raised the piece of silk. "Oh, Mrs. 220 Peters!" she cried. "It's—"

Mrs. Peters bent closer.

"It's the bird," she whispered.

"But, Mrs. Peters!" cried Mrs. Hale. "*Look* at it! Its neck—look at its neck! It's all—other side *to*."

She held the box away from her.

The sheriff's wife again bent closer. 225

"Somebody wrung its neck," said she, in a voice that was slow and deep.

And then again the eyes of the two women met—this time clung together in a look of dawning comprehension, of growing horror. Mrs. Peters looked from the dead bird to the broken door of the cage. Again their eyes met. And just then there was a sound at the outside door.

Mrs. Hale slipped the box under the quilt pieces in the basket, and sank into the chair before it. Mrs. Peters stood holding to the table. The county attorney and the sheriff came in from outside.

"Well, ladies," said the county attorney, as one turning from serious things to little pleasantries, "have you decided whether she was going to quilt it or knot it?"

"We think," began the sheriff's wife in a flurried voice, "that she was 230 going to—knot it."

He was too preoccupied to notice the change that came in her voice on that last.

"Well, that's very interesting, I'm sure," he said tolerantly. He caught sight of the birdcage. "Has the bird flown?"

"We think the cat got it," said Mrs. Hale in a voice curiously even.

He was walking up and down, as if thinking something out.

"Is there a cat?" he asked absently.   235

Mrs. Hale shot a look up at the sheriff's wife.

"Well, not *now*," said Mrs. Peters. "They're superstitious, you know, they leave."

She sank into the chair.

The county attorney did not heed her. "No sign at all of any one having come in from the outside." he said to Peters, in the manner of continuing an interrupted conversation. "Their own rope. Now let's go upstairs again and go over it, piece by piece. It would have to have been some one who knew just the—"

The stair door closed behind them and their voices were lost.   240

The two women sat motionless, not looking at each other, but as if peering into something and at the same time holding back. When they spoke now it was if they were afraid of what they were saying, but as if they could not help saying it.

"She liked the bird," said Martha Hale, low and slowly. "She was going to bury it in that pretty box."

"When I was a girl," said Mrs. Peters, under her breath, "my kitten—there was a boy took a hatchet, and before my eyes—before I could get there—" She covered her face an instant. "If they hadn't held me back I would have"—she caught herself, looked upstairs where footsteps were heard, and finished weakly—"hurt him."

Then they sat without speaking or moving.

"I wonder how it would seem," Mrs. Hale at last began, as if feeling her 245 way over strange ground—"never to have had any children around?" Her eyes made a slow sweep of the kitchen, as if seeing what that kitchen had meant through all the years. "No, Wright wouldn't like the bird," she said after that—"a thing that sang. She used to sing. He killed that too." Her voice tightened.

Mrs. Peters moved uneasily.

"Of course we don't know who killed the bird."

"I knew John Wright," was Mrs. Hale's answer.

"It was an awful thing was done in the house that night, Mrs. Hale," said the sheriff's wife. "Killing a man while he slept—slipping a thing round his neck that choked the life out of him."

Mrs. Hale's hand went out to the birdcage.   250

"His neck. Choked the life out of him."

"We don't *know* who killed him," whispered Mrs. Peters wildly. "We don't *know*."

Mrs. Hale had not moved. "If there had been years and years of—nothing, then a bird to sing to you, it would be awful—still—after the bird was still."

It was as if something within her not herself had spoken, and it found in Mrs. Peters something she did not know as herself.

"I know what stillness is," she said, in a queer, monotonous voice. 255 "When we homesteaded in Dakota, and my first baby died—after he was two years old—and me with no other then—"

Mrs. Hale stirred.

"How soon do you suppose they'll be through looking for evidence?"

"I know what stillness is," repeated Mrs. Peters, in just that same way. Then she too pulled back. "The law has got to punish crime, Mrs. Hale," she said in her tight little way.

"I wish you'd seen Minnie Foster," was the answer, "when she wore a white dress with blue ribbons, and stood up there in the choir and sang."

The picture of that girl, the fact that she had lived neighbor to that girl 260 for twenty years, and had let her die for lack of life, was suddenly more than she could bear.

"Oh, I *wish* I'd come over here once in a while!" she cried. "That was a crime! That was a crime! Who's going to punish that?"

"We mustn't take on," said Mrs. Peters, with a frightened look toward the stairs.

"I might 'a' *known* she needed help! I tell you, it's *queer*, Mrs. Peters. We live close together, and we live far apart. We all go through the same things—it's all just a different kind of the same thing! If it weren't—why do you and I *understand?* Why do we *know*—what we know this minute?"

She dashed her hand across her eyes. Then, seeing the jar of fruit on the table, she reached for it and choked out:

"If I was you I wouldn't *tell* her her fruit was gone! tell her it *ain't*. Tell 265 her it's all right—all of it. Here—take this in to prove it to her! She—she may never know whether it was broke or not."

She turned away.

Mrs. Peters reached out for the bottle of fruit as if she were glad to take it—as if touching a familiar thing, having something to do, could keep her from something else. She got up, looked about for something to wrap the fruit in, took a petticoat from the pile of clothes she had brought from the front room, and nervously started winding that round the bottle.

"My!" she began, in a high, false voice, "it's a good thing the men couldn't hear us! Getting all stirred up over a little thing like a—dead canary." She hurried over that. "As if that could have anything to do with—with—My, wouldn't they *laugh?*"

Footsteps were heard on the stairs.

"Maybe they would," muttered Mrs. Hale—"maybe they wouldn't."   270

"No, Peters," said the county attorney incisively; "it's all perfectly clear, except the reason for doing it. But you know juries when it comes to women. If there was a definite thing—something to show. Something to make a story about. A thing that would connect up with this clumsy way of doing it."

In a covert way Mrs. Hale looked at Mrs. Peters. Mrs. Peters was looking at her. Quickly they looked away from each other. The outer door opened and Mr. Hale came in.

"I've got the team round now," he said. "Pretty cold out there."

"I'm going to stay here awhile by myself," the county attorney suddenly announced. "You can send Frank out for me, can't you?" he asked the sheriff. "I want to go over everything. I'm not satisfied we can't do better."

Again, for one brief moment, the two women's eyes found one another.   275
The sheriff came up to the table.

"Did you want to see what Mrs. Peters was going to take in?"

The county attorney picked up the apron. He laughed.

"Oh, I guess they're not very dangerous things the ladies have picked out."

Mrs. Hale's hand was on the sewing basket in which the box was con-   280
cealed. She felt that she ought to take her hand off the basket. She did not seem able to. He picked up one of the quilt blocks which she had piled on to cover the box. Her eyes felt like fire. She had a feeling that if he took up the basket she would snatch it from him.

But he did not take it up. With another little laugh, he turned away, saying:

"No; Mrs. Peters doesn't need supervising. For that matter, a sheriff's wife is married to the law. Ever think of it that way, Mrs. Peters?"

Mrs. Peters was standing beside the table. Mrs. Hale shot a look up at her, but she could not see her face. Mrs. Peters had turned away. When she spoke, her voice was muffled.

"Not—just that way," she said.

"Married to the law!" chuckled Mrs. Peter's husband. He moved toward **285** the door into the front room, and said to the county attorney:

"I just want you to come in here a minute, George. We ought to take a look at these windows."

"Oh—windows," said the county attorney scoffingly.

"We'll be right out, Mr. Hale," said the sheriff to the farmer, who was still waiting by the door.

Hale went to look after the horses. The sheriff followed the county attorney into the other room. Again—for one moment—the two women were alone in that kitchen.

Martha Hale sprang up, her hands tight together, looking at that other **290** woman, with whom it rested. At first she could not see her eyes, for the sheriff's wife had not turned back since she turned away at that suggestion of being married to the law. But now Mrs. Hale made her turn back. Her eyes made her turn back. Slowly, unwillingly, Mrs. Peters turned her head until her eyes met the eyes of the other woman. There was a moment when they held each other in a steady, burning look in which there was no evasion nor flinching. Then Martha Hale's eyes pointed the way to the basket in which was hidden the thing that would make certain the conviction of the other woman—that woman who was not there and yet who had been there with them all through the hour.

For a moment Mrs. Peters did not move. And then she did it. With a rush forward, she threw back the quilt pieces, got the box, tried to put it in her handbag. It was too big. Desperately she opened it, started to take the bird out. But there she broke—she could not touch the bird. She stood helpless, foolish.

There was the sound of a knob turning in the inner door. Martha Hale snatched the box from the sheriff's wife, and got it in the pocket of her big coat just as the sheriff and the county attorney came back into the kitchen.

"Well, Henry," said the county attorney facetiously, "at least we found out that she was not going to quilt it. She was going to—what is it you call it, ladies?"

Mrs. Hale's hand was against the pocket of her coat.

"We call it—knot it, Mr. Henderson." **295**

LEONARD MUSTAZZA

Generic Translation and Thematic Shift in Susan Glaspell's *Trifles* and "A Jury of Her Peers"

Commentators on Susan Glaspell's classic feminist short story, "A Jury of Her Peers" (1917), and the one-act play from which it derives, *Trifles* (1916), have tended to regard the two works as essentially alike. And even those few who have noticed the changes that Glaspell made in the process of generic translation have done so only in passing. In his monograph on Glaspell, Arthur Waterman, who seems to have a higher regard for the story than for the play, suggests that [the] story is a "moving fictional experience" because of the progressive honing of the author's skills, the story's vivid realism owing to her work as a local-color writer for the *Des Moines Daily News*, and its unified plot due to its dramatic origin (Waterman 29–30). More specifically, Elaine Hedges appropriately notes the significance of Glaspell's change in titles from *Trifles*, which emphasizes the supposedly trivial household items with which the women "acquit" their accused peer, to "A Jury of Her Peers," which emphasizes the question of legality. In 1917, Hedges observes, women were engaged in the final years of their fight for the vote, and Glaspell's change in titles thus "emphasizes the story's comtemporaneity, by calling attention to its references to the issue of women's legal place in American society" (Hedges 106). Apart from these and a few other passing remarks, however, critics have chosen to focus on one work or the other. Indeed, thematic criticisms of the respective pieces are virtually indistinguishable, most of these commentaries focusing on the question of assumed "roles" in the works.[1]

On one level, there is good reason for this lack of differentiation. Not only is the overall narrative movement of the works similar, but Glaspell incorporated in the short story virtually every single line of the dialogue from *Trifles*.[2] By the same token, though, she also added much to the short story, which is about twice as long as the play. The nature of the additions is twofold, the first and most obvious being her descriptions of locales, modes of utterance, characters, props, and so on—the kinds of descriptions that the prose writer's form will allow but the dramatist's will not. The other type of alteration is more subtle, and it involves the revisions, embellishments, and redirections that occur when an existent story is retold. When, for instance, a novel is turned into a film of a play, the best that can be said about the generic translation is that it is "faithful," but never is it identical. So it is with "Jury." It is certainly faithful to the play, but it is also different in a variety of ways, and it is these differences, which took place in the act of generic translation, that I would like to consider here.

In her articles on *Trifles*, Beverly Smith makes an interesting observation. Noting that the women in the play, Mrs. Hale and Mrs. Peters, function as defense counsel for and jury of their accused peer, Minnie Foster Wright, she goes on to suggest that the men's role, their official capacities notwithstanding, are comparable to that of a Greek Chorus, "the voice of the community's conscience," entering at various points to reiterate their major themes—Minnie's guilt and the triviality of the women's occupations, avocations, and preoccupations (Smith 175). This equation is, I think, quite useful, for the periodic entries, commentaries, and exits of the male characters in both Glaspell works do in fact mark the progressive stages of the narrative, which primarily concerns the women, including the absent Minnie Foster.[3] Though not on stage for the entire drama, as is the Greek Chorus, the men nevertheless function in much the same way, providing commentary and separating the major movements of the narrative. What is more, if we regard the men's exits from the stage as marking these movements, we will recognize the first principal difference between the play and the story—namely, that the latter contains twice as many movements as the former and is therefore necessarily a more developed and complex work.

Trifles opens with Mr. Hale's account of what he found when he arrived at the Wright farm the day before. Of the women themselves, we know almost nothing beyond their general appearances as described in the opening stage directions—that Mrs. Peters, the sheriff's wife, is "a slight, wiry woman [with] a thin nervous face"; and that Mrs. Hale, the witness's wife, is larger than Mrs. Peters and "comfortable looking," though now appearing fearful and disturbed as she enters the scene of the crime (Glaspell, *Trifles* 15). Standing close together as they enter the Wright's home, the women remain almost completely undifferentiated until, some time later, they begin to speak. Thus, Glaspell underscores here the male/female polarities that she will explore in the course of the play.

Her entire narrative technique is different in the prose version. That story begins in Mrs. Hale's disordered kitchen, which will later serve as a point of comparison with the major scene of the story, Mrs. Wright's kitchen. Annoyed at being called away from her housework, she nevertheless agrees to Sheriff Peter's request that she come along to accompany Mrs. Peters, who is there to fetch some personal effects for the jailed woman. Quite unlike the play's opening, which emphasizes the physical closeness of and the attitudinal similarities between the women, "Jury," taking us as it does into Mrs. Hale's thoughts, emphasizes the women's apartness:

> She had met Mrs. Peters the year before at the county fair, and the thing she remembered about her was that *she didn't seem like the sheriff's wife*. She was small and thin and didn't have a strong voice. Mrs. Gorman, the sheriff's wife before Gorman went out and Peters came in, had a voice that somehow seemed to be backing up the law with every word. But if Mrs. Peters didn't look like a sheriff's wife, Peters made up for it in looking like a sheriff—a heavy man with a big voice, who was particularly genial with the law-abiding, as if to make it plain that he knew the difference between criminals and non-criminals. (Glaspell, "Jury" 70; emphasis added)

Interestingly, for all the added material here, Glaspell omits mention of what the women look like. In fact, we will get no explicit statements on their appearance.

Ironically, however despite her seeming mismatch with her husband, her lack of corporeal "presence," Mrs. Peters turns out to be more suited to her assumed public role than Mrs. Hale had suspected—all too suited, in fact, since she perfectly assumes her male-approved role. "Of course Mrs. Peters is one of us" (77), the county attorney asserts prior to getting on with his investigation of the house, and that statement turns out to be laden with meaning in the story. In *Trifles*, when the men leave to go about their investigative business, the women, we are told, "listen to the men's steps, then look about the kitchen" (19). In "Jury," however, we get much more. Again here, the women stand motionless, listening to the men's footsteps, but this momentary stasis is followed by a significant gesture: "Then, *as if releasing herself from something strange*, Mrs. Hale began to arrange the dirty pans under the sink, which the county attorney's disdainful push of the foot had deranged" (77; emphasis added). One is prompted here to ask: what is this "something strange" from which she releases herself? Though the actions described in the play and the story are the same, why does Glaspell not include in the stage directions to the play an indication of Mrs. Hale's facial expression?

The answer, I think, lies again in the expanded and altered context of "Jury," where the author continually stresses the distance between the women. If Mrs. Peters is, as the county attorney has suggested, one of "them," Mrs. Hale certainly is not, and she distances herself from her male-approved peer in word and deed. The something strange from which she releases herself is, in this context, her reflexive movement towards Mrs. Peters. Mrs. Hale is, in fact, both extricating herself from the male strictures placed upon all of the women and asserting her intellectual independence. Karen Alkalay-Gut has correctly observed that, to the men, the disorder of Mrs. Wright's kitchen implies her "potential homicidal tendencies, inconceivable in a good wife" (3). For her part, Mrs. Hale is rejecting the men's specious reasoning, complaining about the lawyer's disdainful treatment of the kitchen things and asserting, "I'd hate to have men comin' into my kitchen, snoopin' round and criticizin' " (77), obviously recalling the disorder in her kitchen and resenting the conclusions about her that could be drawn. Lacking that opening scene, the play simply does not resonate so profoundly.

Even more telling is a subtle but important change that Glaspell made following Mrs. Hale's testy assertion. In both the play and the story, Mrs. Peters offers the meek defense, "Of course it's no more than their duty" (*Trifles*, 19; "Jury," 77), and then the two works diverge. In *Trifles*, Mrs. Peters manages to change the subject. Noticing some dough that Mrs. Wright had been preparing the day before, she says flatly, "she had bread set" (20), and that statement directs Mrs. Hale's attention to the half-done and ruined kitchen chores. In effect, the flow of conversation is mutually directed in the play, and the distance between the women is thus minimized. When she wrote the story, however, Glaspell omitted mention of the bread and instead took us into Mrs. Hale's thoughts, as she does at the beginning of the story:

> She thought of the flour in her kitchen at home—half sifted, half not sifted. She had been interrupted, and had left things half done. What had interrupted Minnie Foster? Why had that work been left half done? She made a move as if to finish it,—unfinished things always bothered her,—and then she glanced around and saw that Mrs. Peters was watching her—and she didn't want Mrs. Peters to get that feeling she got of work begun and then—for some reason—not finished.
> "It's a shame about her fruit," she said . . . .(77–78)

Although mention of the ruined fruit preserved is included in the play as well, two significant additions are made in the above passage. First, there is the continual comparison between Mrs. Hale's life and Mrs. Wright's. Second, and more important, we get the clear sense here of Mrs. Hale's suspicion of Mrs. Peters, her not wanting to call attention to the unfinished job for fear that the sheriff's wife will get the wrong idea—or, in this case, the right idea, for the evidence of disturbance, however circumstantial, is something the men may be able to use against Mrs. Wright. In other words, unlike the play, the story posits a different set of polarities, with Mrs. Peters presumably occupying a place within the official party and Mrs. Hale taking the side of the accused against all of them.

We come at this point to a crossroads in the story. Mrs. Hale can leave things as they are and keep information to herself, or she can recruit Mrs. Peters as a fellow "juror" in the case, moving the sheriff's wife away from her sympathy for her husband's position and towards identification with the accused woman. Mrs. Hale chooses the latter course and sets about persuading Mrs. Peters to emerge, in Alkalay-Gut's words, "as an individual distinct from her role as sheriff's wife." Once that happens, "her identification with Minnie is rapid and becomes complete" (6).

The persuasive process begins easily but effectively, with Mrs. Hale reflecting upon the change in Minnie Foster Wright over the thirty or so years she has known her—the change, to use the metaphor that Glaspell will develop, from singing bird to muted caged bird. She follows this reminiscence with a direct question to Mrs. Peters about whether the latter thinks that Minnie killed her husband. "Oh, I don't know," is the frightened response in both works (*Trifles*, 21; "Jury," 79), but, as always, the story provides more insight and tension than does the drama. Still emphasizing in her revision the distance between the two women, Glaspell has Mrs. Hale believe that her talk of the youthful Minnie has fallen on deaf ears: "Much difference it makes to her whether Minnie Foster had pretty clothes when she was a girl" (78). This sense of the other woman's indifference to such irrelevant trivialities is occasioned not only by Mrs. Hale's persistent belief in the other woman's official role but also by an odd look that crosses Mrs. Peters' face. At the second glance, however, Mrs. Hale notices something else that melts her annoyance and undercuts her suspicions about the sheriff's wife: "Then she looked again, and she wasn't so sure; in fact, she hadn't at any time been perfectly sure about Mrs. Peters. She had that shrinking manner, and yet her eyes looked as if they could see a long way into things" (79). Whereas the play shows the women meandering towards concurrence, the short story is here seen to evolve—and part of that evolution, we must conclude, is due to Mrs. Hale's ability to persuade her peer to regard the case from her perspective. The look that she sees in Mrs. Peters' eyes suggests to her that she might be able to persuade her, that the potential for identification is there. Hence, when she asks whether Mrs. Peters thinks Minnie is guilty, the question resonates here in ways the play does not.

Accordingly, Mrs. Hale will become much more aggressive in her arguments hereafter, taking on something of the persuader's hopeful hostility, which, in the case of the story, stands in marked contrast to the hostility she felt for Mrs. Peters' official role earlier. Thus, when Mrs. Peters tries to retreat into a male argument, weakly asserting that "the law is the law," (*Trifles*, 22; "Jury," 80), the Mrs. Hale of the short story does not let the remark pass, as the one in *Trifles* does: "the law is the law—and a bad stove is a bad stove. How'd you like to cook on this?" Even she, however, is startled by Mrs. Peters' immediate response to her homey analogy and *ad hominem* attack: "A person gets discouraged—and loses heart," Mrs. Peters says—"That look of seeing . . . through a thing to something else" (80) back on her face.

As far as I am concerned, the addition of this passage is the most important change that Glaspell made in her generic translation. Having used this direct personal attack and having noted the ambivalence that Mrs. Peters feels for her role as sheriff's wife, Mrs. Hale will now proceed to effect closure of the gap between them—again, a gap that is never this widely opened in *Trifles*. Now Mrs. Hale will change her entire mode of attack, pushing the limits, doing things she hesitated doing earlier, assailing Mrs. Peters whenever she lapses into her easy conventional attitudes. For instance, when Mrs. Peters objects to Mrs. Hale's repair of a badly knitted quilt block—in effect, tampering with circumstantial evidence of Minnie's mental disturbance the day before—Mrs. Hale proceeds to do it anyway. As a measure of how much she has changed, we have only to compare this act with her earlier hesitation to finish another chore for fear of what Mrs. Peters might think. She has no reason to be distrustful of Mrs. Peters any longer, for the process of identification is now well underway.

That identification becomes quite evident by the time the women find the most compelling piece of circumstantial evidence against Mrs. Wright—the broken bird cage and the dead bird, its neck wrung and its body placed in a pretty box in Mrs. Wright's sewing basket. When the men notice the cage and Mrs. Hale misleadingly speculates that a cat may have been at it, it is Mrs. Peters who confirms the matter. Asked by the county attorney whether a cat was on the premises, Mrs. Peters—fully aware that there is no cat and never has been—quickly and evasively replies, "Well not *now* . . . . They're superstitious, you know; they leave" (85). Not only is Mrs. Peters deliberately lying here, but, more important, she is assuming quite another role from the one she played earlier. Uttering a banality, she plays at being the shallow woman who believes in superstitions, thus consciously playing one of the roles the men expect her to assume and concealing her keen intellect from them, her ability to extrapolate facts from small details. From this point forward, the play and the short story are essentially the same. Mrs. Hale will continue her persuasive assault, and Mrs. Peters will continue to struggle inwardly. The culmination of this struggle occurs when, late in the story, the county sheriff says that "a sheriff's wife is married to the law," and she responds, "Not—just that way" (*Trifles*, 27; "Jury," 88). In "Jury," however, this protest carries much greater force than it does in *Trifles* for the simple reason that it is a measure of how far Mrs. Peters has come in the course of the short story.

Appropriately enough, too, Mrs. Hale has the final word in both narratives. Asked derisively by the county attorney what stitch Mrs. Wright had been using to make her quilt, Mrs. Hale responds with false sincerity, "We call it—knot it, Mr. Henderson" (*Trifles*, 28; "Jury," 88). Most critics have read this line as an ironic reference to the women's solidarity at this point.[4] That is quite true, but, as I have been suggesting here, the progress towards this solidarity varies subtly but unmistakably in the two narratives. Whereas *Trifles*, opening as it does with the women's close physical proximity, reveals the dichotomy between male and female concepts of justice and social roles, "A Jury of Her Peers" is much more concerned with the separateness of the women themselves and their self-injurious acquiescence in male-defined roles. Hence, in her reworking of the narrative, Glaspell did much more than translate the material from one genre to another. Rather, she subtly changed its theme, and, in so doing, she wrote a story that is much more interesting, resonant, and disturbing than the slighter drama from which it derives.

NOTES

1. Rachel France notes that *Trifles* reveals "the dichotomy between men and women in rural life," an important feature of that dichotomy being the men's "proclivity for the letter of the law" as opposed to the women's more humane understanding of justice ("Apropos of Women and the Folk Play," in *Women in American Theatre: Careers, Images, Movements*, ed. Helen Krich Chinoy and Linda Walsh Jenkins [New York: Crown, 1981], p. 151). Karen Alkalay-Gut observes three polarities in "Jury": the opposition between the large external male world and the women's more circumscribed place within the home; the attitudes of men and women generally; and the distinction between *law*, which is identified with "the imposition of abstractions on individual circumstances," and *justice*, "the extrapolation of judgment from individual circumstances" ("'A Jury of Her Peers': The Importance of *Trifles*," *Studies in Short Fiction*, 21 [Winter 1984], 2). Karen Stein

calls the play "an anomaly in the murder mystery genre, which is predominantly a male tour de force." By bonding together, she goes on, the women act in a manner that is "diametrically opposed to the solo virtuosity usually displayed by male detectives" ("The Women's World of Glaspell's *Trifles*," in *Women in American Theatre*, ed. Helen Krich Chinoy and Linda Walsh Jenkins [New York: Crown, 1981], p. 254). Judith Fetterley also advances an interesting and imaginative interpretation. She sees the characters in "Jury" as readers and the trivial household items as their text. The men fail to read the same meanings in that text that the women do because they are committed to "the equation of textuality with masculine subject matter and masculine point of view" ("Reading about Reading: 'A Jury of Her Peers,' 'The Murders in the Rue Morgue,' and 'The Yellow Wallpaper,'" in *Gender and Reading: Essays on Readers, Texts and Contexts*, ed. Elizabeth A. Flynn and Patrocinio P. Schweickart [Baltimore: Johns Hopkins Univ. Press, 1986], pp. 147–48).

2. Elaine Hedges notes that one reference included in the play but omitted from "Jury" is Mrs. Hale's lament that, because of Mr. Wright's parsimony, Minnie could not join the Ladies' Aid, a society in which women cooperated with the local church to make items like carpets and quilts. These items were then sold to support ministers' salaries and to aid foreign missions. Minnie is thus denied not only the company of other women but also one of the few public roles that farm women were allowed to play ("Small Things Reconsidered," p. 102). In this regard, the story reveals, as Jeannie McKnight suggests, "a kind of classic 'cabin fever' as motivation for the homicide . . . " ("American Dream, Nightmare Underside: Diaries, Letters, and Fiction of Women on the American Frontier," in *Women, Women Writers, and the West*, ed. L. L. Lee and Merrill Lewis [Troy, NY: Whitson, 1979], p. 31).

3. Cynthia Sutherland aptly observes that the story's effect depends to a large extent upon the removal of Minnie from the sight of the audience, thus focusing our attention on the facts of her plight rather than on her appearance and mannerisms ("American Women Playwrights as Mediators of the 'Woman Problem,'" *Modern Drama*, 21 [September 1978], 323).

4. Beverly Smith sees "the bond among women [as] the essential knot" ("Women's Work," p. 179). Cynthia Sutherland regards the reference to knotting as "a subdued, ironic, and grisly reminder of the manner in which a stifled wife has enacted her desperate retaliation" ("American Women Playwrights," p. 323). And Elaine Hedges argues that the reference has three meanings: the rope that Minnie knotted around her husband's neck; the bond among the women; and the fact that the women have tied the men in knots ("Small Things Reconsidered," p. 107).

WORKS CITED

Alkalay-Gut, Karen. "'A Jury of Her Peers': The Importance of *Trifles*." Studies in Short Fiction 21 (Winter 1984): 1–9.

Glaspell, Susan. "A Jury of Her Peers." The Wadsworth Casebook Series for Reading, Research, and Writing: Trifles. Ed. Donna Winchell. Boston: Wadsworth, 2004. 70–88.

———. *Trifles*. The Wadsworth Casebook Series for Reading, Research, and Writing: Trifles. Ed. Donna Winchell. Boston: Wadsworth, 2004. 15–28.

Hedges, Elaine. "Small Things Reconsidered: Susan Glaspell's 'A Jury of Her Peers.'" Women's Studies 12.1 (1986): 89–110.

Smith, Beverly, A. "Women's Work—*Trifles*? The Skill and Insight of Playwright Susan Glaspell." International Journal of Women's Studies 5 (March–April 1982): 175.

Waterman, Arthur E. Susan Glaspell. New York: Twayne, 1966.

Sample Student Research Paper

Kelli Bolt

Professor Winchell

Literature I

June 3, 2003

Surrogate Jurors

Some plays withstand better than others the test of time.
Susan Glaspell wrote her play *Trifles* in 1916 while she was
part of a group of playwrights and actors in Massachusetts
called the Provincetown Players. As long ago as 1916 may seem
to us living in the early 21st century, Linda Ben-Zvi writes
in her essay "'Murder She Wrote': The Genesis of Susan
Glaspell's *Trifles*" that it is either "a testament to the
skill with which Glaspell constructed *Trifles* . . . or proof
of how little women's lives have changed since 1916" that
feminist critics still consider the play important because it
anticipated later plays about feminist issues (46). Glaspell
wrote the play to address directly a specific women's problem
that would not have been lost on her audience. In 1916, women
did not have the right to serve on juries (Ben-Zvi 44); for
that matter, it would be four years before they possessed
the right to vote. With *Trifles*, Glaspell illustrates the
absurdity of the situation in which women are judged and
convicted solely by men.

    The men in the play represent the male-dominated system
in which women are forced to live, but these men cannot
comprehend what would motivate a woman to commit murder in
such a system. Unable to understand a woman's motivation
and, most important, the frustration that is a major component
of that motivation, the three male characters — Mr. Hale, Sheriff
Peters, and the county attorney, George Henderson — fail

Introduction provides historical context

Thesis statement

Sets up contrast between men's and women's ability to understand the murder

Bolt 2

miserably in their search for Minnie Wright's motivation for her husband's murder. Only when the men leave the action of the play to go upstairs and investigate the crime scene are the women able to focus on the real subject at hand: the life of Minnie Wright.

Mr. Hale says, "Well, women are used to worrying over trifles" (Glaspell 18). On the most obvious level, he is referring to Mrs. Hale and Mrs. Peters's concern for whether or not Minnie Wright's preserves have survived the freezing temperatures in the unheated house. On a deeper level, the two women's worry over Minnie Wright's miserable life is just another "trifle" to the men. Minnie, herself, has been reduced to a name. She is not even physically present throughout the play (Alkalay-Gut 52). Because Minnie's entire existence has been reduced to a world composed of such "trifles" as the men chuckle about, it is only the women who will understand the truth behind the investigation, for they also live with such "trifles." Mrs. Peters and Mrs. Hale understand the desperation that can result from being completely isolated in such a lonely and bleak world. These women realize that the isolation Minnie faced would be reflected in the "trappings" of domestic life to which she was limited. In other words, the women are the only capable judges in the house because they are limited, though perhaps not as harshly, as Minnie Wright was herself.

More detailed support for why the women but not the men can identify with Mrs. Wright.

It is within these limitations that Mrs. Hale and Mrs. Peters begin to understand the psychological motivation behind Minnie's actions. Even if the men suspected that Mrs. Wright's husband was somehow responsible for his wife's actions, these suspicions would be erased quickly by fear and denial. As Ben-Zvi states in her essay, "Women who kill evoke fear because they challenge societal constructs of femininity—passivity, restraint, and nurture—thus the rush to isolate and

How society's views of gender roles keep women off juries.

Bolt 3

label the female offender, to cauterize the act" (33). As
"pillars of the community," these men are faced with the
"responsibility" of upholding societal expectations of
femininity. In her essay "*Trifles*: The Path to Sisterhood,"
Phyllis Mael writes that Sigmund Freud basically stated that
men have a better sense of justice because they are less
influenced by their relationships. Instead, they have a more
highly developed sense of a separate self and are able to judge
situations from a less subjective point of view. These
observations were made from the perspective that male moral
development is more advanced and female morality somehow "less"
advanced (61). Assumptions of this kind keep women like Mrs.
Hale and Mrs. Peters off a lawful jury in Minnie Wright's
trial.

Since the women are denied the legal right to sit on
a jury and judge their acquaintance, they must take matters
into their own hands, and literally, they do take the

> Therefore, the women decide to serve as informal judge and jury

matter, or the evidence, into hand. The men are too caught up
in their detective game to notice that the real crime scene is
not upstairs; rather, the true crime scene is tucked away in
Minnie Wright's mind, and the evidence of her tormented mind
is lying around the scene of "domestic bliss," the kitchen.

The familiar items that the Mrs. Hale and Mrs. Peters
find in Minnie Wright's kitchen—jars of preserves, uncooked

> What qualifies them as "jurors"

bread, and the beginnings of a quilt—all create a bond among
the three women. Because Mrs. Hale and Mrs. Peters have spent
so much of their own lives surrounded by these things, they are
able, unlike the men who take them for granted, to read each
item's significance. In other words, as Phyllis Mael points
out, the women are able to apply their own version of feminine
developmental psychology: "Current feminist research in
developmental psychology can help increase our admiration for

Bolt 4

Glaspell's challenging presentation of the moral dilemma and
the way in which Minnie's trifles raise the consciousness of
both women . . . , moving them from awareness to anger to action"
(61). Mrs. Hale and Mrs. Peters have begun to challenge the
idea of what is aberrant female behavior and what is simply a
response to personal environment, as was the case with Minnie
Wright.

Just as psychoanalysis is sometimes based heavily on
the symbolism of objects and actions, Glaspell's *Trifles* is
also filled with symbols of Minnie's entrapment in her rural
environment. There are the crooked stitching on the "log
cabin" design quilt piece, the dead canary, the broken jars
of preserves, the uncooked bread, and the worn clothes of Mrs.
Wright. All of these things symbolize a life that is somehow
undone, shattered, or defeated. The men comment on the
condition of the hand towels in the kitchen. Mrs. Hale is quick
to point out, "Men's hands aren't always as clean as they might
be" (19). In other words, the men have entered Minnie Wright's
kitchen under the assumption that a woman who kills her husband
is always at fault, and the husband's hands must be clean of
the matter. Mrs. Hale knows better. She knows that all men bear
some responsibility in a wife's misery.

Symbols of the mistreatment that led Mrs. Wright to murder — the "evidence" in her trial.

The symbolism in *Trifles* is not hard to decipher, just
as the significance of the play itself, in terms of women's
rights, would not have been hard for Glaspell's audience to
interpret. Undoubtedly, Glaspell set out to make a bold
statement with *Trifles*, and she succeeded. Veronica Makowsky
writes, "Glaspell and her fellow artists operated under the
premise that art and life were inextricably linked . . . .
Glaspell's women protagonists . . . attempt to bring the best
parts of the past forward while attempting to create new forms
in the present that will, in turn, benefit the future" (50).

Art and life are linked for both Mrs. Wright and her creator

Bolt 5

The idea that art and life are linked is illustrated both by
the play and by Glaspell's life as an artist. The erratic
stitching on Minnie's quilt, perhaps her only creative outlet,
reflects the torment that her husband inflicted upon her. In
other words, Minnie's "art" reflects her life. Glaspell's art,
her writing, is used to better the lives of women. In writing
Trifles, Glaspell was and is able to make a statement about the
restriction on women jurors. She is also able to make an
overall statement about how far women have come and still need
to go in the struggle for women's rights.

As women continue to advance, perhaps Glaspell's name
will gain ground in terms of becoming more familiar to
readers. As Barbara Ozieblo points out in her essay

Links restrictions on Mrs. Wright to those on Glaspell as a writer.

"Rebellion and Rejection: The Plays of Susan Glaspell," it is
plausible that Glaspell has been kept out of the canon in the
past because her strong "female characters threaten patriarchal
power" (66). Perhaps with the progress that continues to be
made in women's rights, more readers will begin to understand
that a writer of such rich talent and influence should not be
ignored but welcomed and promoted within the canon of American
literature.

Bolt 6

Works Cited

Alkalay-Gut, Karen. "Murder and Marriage: Another Look at
　　Trifles." The Wadsworth Casebook Series for Reading,
　　Research, and Writing: Trifles. Ed. Donna Winchell. Boston:
　　Wadsworth, 2004. 51-60.

Ben-Zvi, Linda. "'Murder, She Wrote': The Genesis of Susan
　　Glaspell's *Trifles*." The Wadsworth Casebook Series for
　　Reading, Research, and Writing: Trifles. Ed. Donna
　　Winchell. Boston: Wadsworth, 2004. 33-50.

Glaspell, Susan. *Trifles*. The Wadsworth Casebook Series for
　　Reading, Research, and Writing: Trifles. Ed. Donna
　　Winchell. Boston: Wadsworth, 2004. 15-28.

Mael, Phyllis. "*Trifles*: The Path to Sisterhood." The Wadsworth
　　Casebook Series for Reading, Research, and Writing:
　　Trifles. Ed. Donna Winchell. Boston: Wadsworth, 2004.
　　60-65.

Makowsky, Veronica. "Susan Glaspell and Modernism." The
　　Cambridge Companion to American Women Playwrights. Ed.
　　Brenda Murphy. Cambridge [England]; New York: Cambridge UP,
　　1999. 49-65.

Ozieblo, Barbara. "Rebellion and Rejection: The Plays of Susan
　　Glaspell." Modern American Drama: The Female Canon. Ed.
　　June Schlueter. London: Associated UP. 1990. 66-76.

Bibliography

Works by Susan Glaspell

PLAYS

Alison's House: A Play in Three Acts. New York: French, 1930.

Bernice. Plays. Boston: Small, 1920. 157–230.

Chains of Dew. Unpublished.

Close the Book. Plays. Boston: Small, 1920. 61–96.

The Comic Artist: A Play in Three Acts (with Norman Matson). London: Benn, 1927.

Inheritors. Plays by Susan Glaspell. Ed. C. W. E. Bigsby. Cambridge: Cambridge UP, 1987. 103–57.

The Outside. Plays. Boston: Small, 1920. Rpt. in Plays by Susan Glaspell. Ed. C. W. E. Bigsby. Cambridge: Cambridge UP, 1987. 47–55.

The People. Plays. Boston: Small, 1920. 31–60.

Plays. Boston: Small, 1920.

Plays by Susan Glaspell. Ed. C. W. E. Bigsby. Cambridge: Cambridge UP, 1987.

Suppressed Desires. Plays. Boston: Small, 1920. 231–72.

Tickless Time. Plays. Boston: Small, 1920. 273–315.

Trifles. Plays. Boston: Small, 1920. Rpt. in Plays by Susan Glaspell. Ed. C. W. E. Bigsby. Cambridge: Cambridge UP, 1987. 35–45.

The Verge. Plays by Susan Glaspell. Ed. C. W. E. Bigsby. Cambridge: Cambridge UP, 1987. 57–101.

Woman's Honor. Plays. Boston: Small, 1920. 119–56.

NOVELS

Ambrose Holt and Family. New York: Stokes, 1931.

Brook Evans. New York: Stokes, 1928.

Cherished and Shared of Old. New York: Messner, 1940.

Fidelity. Boston: Small, 1915.

Fugitive's Return. New York: Stokes, 1929.

The Glory of the Conquered: The Story of a Great Love. New York: Stokes, 1909.

Judd Rankin's Daughter. New York: Lippincott, 1945.

The Morning Is Near Us. New York: Stokes, 1939.

Norma Ashe. New York: Lippincott, 1942.

The Visioning. New York: Stokes, 1911.

BIOGRAPHY

The Road to the Temple. New York: Stokes, 1927.

SHORT STORIES

Lifted Mask and Other Works. Introduction by Eric S. Rabkin. 1912. Ann Arbor: U of Michigan P, 1993.

Works of General Interest about Susan Glaspell

Andrews, Clarence, and Marcia Noe. "Susan Glaspell of Davenport." The Iowan 25 (Summer 1977): 46–53.

Bach, Gerhard. "Susan Glaspell: A Bibliography of Dramatic Criticism." Great Lakes Review 3.2 (1977): 1–34.

———. "Susan Glaspell: Provincetown Playwright." Great Lakes Review 4.2 (1978): 31–43.

Ben-Zvi, Linda. "Susan Glaspell: A Biographical Essay." Notable Women in American Theatre. Ed. Vera Roberts et al. Westport: Greenwood, 1990. 341–46.

———. "Susan Glaspell and Eugene O'Neill." Eugene O'Neill Newsletter 6.2 (1982): 21–29.

———. "Susan Glaspell and Eugene O'Neill: The Imagery of Gender." Eugene O'Neill Newsletter 10.1 (1986): 22–27.

———. "Susan Glaspell's Contributions to Modern Women Playwrights." Feminine Focus. Ed. Enoch Brater. New York: Oxford UP, 1987. 147–66.

Bigsby, C. W. E. "Introduction." Susan Glaspell: Plays. Cambridge: Cambridge UP, 1987. 1–31.

———. "Provincetown: The Birth of Twentieth-Century American Drama." A Critical Introduction to Twentieth Century American Drama: Vol. 1, 1900–1940. Cambridge: Cambridge UP., 1982. 1–35.

Dymkowski, Christine. "On the Edge: The Plays of Susan Glaspell." Modern Drama 31 (March 1988): 91–105.

Friedman, Sharon. "Feminism as Theme in Twentieth-Century American Women's Drama." American Studies 25 (Spring 1984): 69–89.

Gould, Jean. "Susan Glaspell and the Provincetown Players." In Modern American Playwrights. New York: Dodd, 1966. 26–49.

Kolodny, Annette. "A Map for Rereading: Or, Gender and the Interpretation of Literary Texts." New Literary History 11 (Spring 1980): 451–67. Rpt. in The New Feminist Criticism: Essays on Women, Literature, and Theory. Ed. Elaine Showalter. New York: Pantheon, 1985. 46–62.

Larabee, Ann E. "Death in Delphi: Susan Glaspell and the Companionate Marriage." Mid American Review 7.2 (1987): 93–106.

Lewisohn, Ludwig. Expression in America. New York: Harper, 1932.

Makowsky, Veronica. Susan Glaspell's Century of American Women: A Critical Interpretation of Her Work. New York: Oxford UP, 1993.

Noe, Marcia. "Region as Metaphor in the Plays of Susan Glaspell." Western Illinois Regional Studies 4.1 (1981): 77–85.

———. Susan Glaspell: Voice from the Heartland. Western Illinois Monograph Series, No. 1. Macomb: Western Illinois P, 1983.

———. "Susan Glaspell's Analysis of the Midwestern Character." Books at Iowa 27 (1977): 3–20.

Ozieblo, Barbara. "Rebellion and Rejection: The Plays of Susan Glaspell." Modern American Drama: The Female Canon. Ed. June Schlueter. Rutherford: Fairleigh Dickinson UP, 1990.

———. Susan Glaspell: A Critical Biography. Chapel Hill: U of North Carolina P, 2000.

Papke, Mary. Susan Glaspell: A Research and Production Sourcebook. Westport: Greenwood, 1993.

Sarlos, Robert K. Jig Cook and the Provincetown Players: Theatre in Ferment. Amherst: U of Massachusetts P, 1982.

Shafer, Yvonne. "Susan Glaspell: German Influence, American Playwright." Zeitschrift fur Anglistik und Amerikanistik 36.4 (1988): 333–38.

Waterman, Arthur E. Susan Glaspell. New York: Twayne, 1966.

———. "Susan Glaspell and the Provincetown." Modern Drama 7 (1964): 174–84.

Critical Appraisals of *Trifles* and "A Jury of Her Peers"

Ben-Zvi, Linda, ed. Susan Glaspell: Essays on Her Theater and Fiction. Ann Arbor: U of Michigan P, 1995.

Carpentier, Martha C. "The Burial and Resurrection of a Writer." In The Major Novels of Susan Glaspell. Gainesville: UP of Florida, 2001.

Fetterley, Judith. "Reading about Reading: 'A Jury of Her Peers,' 'Murder in the Rue Morgue,' and 'The Yellow Wallpaper.' " Gender and Reading: Essays on Readers. Texts and Contexts. Ed. Elizabeth A. Flynn and Patricinio P. Schweickart. Baltimore: Johns Hopkins UP, 1986. 147–64.

Flavin, Louise. " 'A Jury of Her Peers' Needs a Jury of Its Peers." Teaching English in the Two-Year College 10 (Spring 1984): 259–60.

Gubar, Susan, and Anne Hedin. " 'A Jury of Her Peers': Teaching and Learning in the Indiana Women's Prison." College English 43 (1981): 779–89.

Hedges, Elaine. "Small Things Reconsidered: Susan Glaspell's 'A Jury of Her Peers.' " Women's Studies 12.1 (1986): 89–110.

Mael, Phyllis. "*Trifles*: The Path to Sisterhood." Literature/Film Quarterly 17.4 (1989): 281–84.

Makowski, Veronica. "Susan Glaspell and Modernism." The Cambridge Companion to American Women Playwrights. Ed. Brenda Murphy. Cambridge [England]; New York: Cambridge UP, 1999.

Mustazza, Leonard. "Gender and Justice in Susan Glaspell's 'A Jury of Her Peers.'" Law and Semiotics 2 (1988): 271–76.

———. "Generic Translation and Thematic Shift in Susan Glaspell's *Trifles* and 'A Jury of Her Peers.'" Studies in Short Fiction 26.4 (1989): 489–96.

Newman, Kathy. "Susan Glaspell and *Trifles*: 'Nothing Here but Kitchen Things.'" Trivia: A Journal of Ideas (Fall 1983): 88–94.

Stein, Karen F. "The Women's World of Glaspell's *Trifles*." In Women in American Theatre. Ed. Helen Krich Chinoy and Linda Walsh Jenkins. New York: Theatre Communications, 1987.

Film Adaptation

Heckel, Sally, dir. A Jury of Her Peers. Texture Films, 1991.

World Wide Web Sites

American Literature–Research and Analysis Web Site. Ed. Jim Wohlpart. 1997. 9 June 2003 <http://itech.fgcu.edu/faculty/wohlpart/alra/glaspell.htm#Contents>. Path: Susan Glaspell.

Susan Glaspell. Ed. Amari Verastegui. 1999. 9 June 2003 <http://www.tcnj.edu/~verasteg/glaspell.htm>.

Trifles Forum. Ed. Eric Hibbison. May 2003. J. Sargeant Reynolds Community Coll. 9 June 2003 <http://vccslitonline.cc.va.us/Trifles/>.

Susan Glaspell (1876-1948). Ed. Arthur Waterman. 9 June 2003 <http://www.georgetown.edu/faculty/bassr/heath/syllabuild/iguide/glaspell.html>.

American Literature on the Web: Susan Glaspell. Ed. Akihito Ishikawa. Nov. 1999. Nagasaki U of Foreign Studies. 9 June 2003 <http://www.nagasaki- gaigo.ac.jp/ishikawa/amlit/g/glaspell20.htm>.

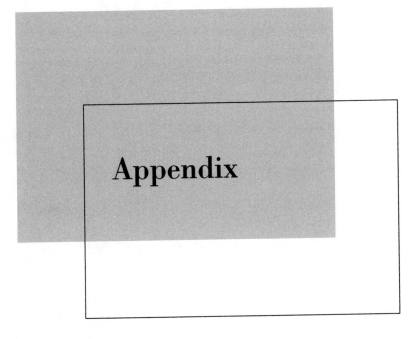

Appendix

A Guide to MLA Documentation Style

Documentation is the acknowledgment of information from outside sources that you use in your paper. In general, give credit to your sources whenever you quote, paraphrase, summarize, or in any way incorporate borrowed information or ideas into your work. Not to do so—on purpose or by accident—is to commit **plagiarism,** to appropriate the intellectual property of others. By following accepted conventions of documentation, you not only help avoid plagiarism, but you show your readers that you write with care and precision. In addition, you enable them to distinguish your ideas from those of your sources and, if they wish, to locate and consult the sources you cite.

Not all ideas from your sources need to be documented. You can assume that certain information—facts from encyclopedias, textbooks, newspapers, magazines, and dictionaries, or even from television and radio—is common knowledge. Even if the information is new to you, it need not be documented as long as it is found in several reference sources and as long as you do not use the exact wording of your source. Information that is in dispute or that is the original contribution of a particular person, however, *must* be documented. You need not, for example, document the fact that Arthur Miller's *Death of a Salesman* was first performed in 1949 or that it won a Pulitzer Prize for drama. (You could find this information in any current encyclopedia.) You would, however, have to document a critic's interpretation of a performance or a scholar's analysis of an early draft of the play, even if you do not use your source's exact words.

Students writing about literature use the documentation style recommended by the Modern Language Association (MLA), a professional organization of more than 25,000 teachers and students of English and other languages. This style of documentation has three parts: *parenthetical references* in the text, a *works-cited list* at the end of the paper, and *content notes.*

PARENTHETICAL REFERENCES IN THE TEXT

MLA documentation style uses parenthetical references within the text to refer to an alphabetical works-cited list at the end of the paper. A parenthetical reference should contain just enough information to guide readers to the appropriate entry on your works-cited list. A typical

parenthetical reference consists of the author's last name and a page number.

> Gwendolyn Brooks uses the sonnet form to create poems that have a wide social and aesthetic range (Williams 972).

If you use more than one source by the same author, include a shortened title in the parenthetical reference.

> Brooks knows not only Shakespeare, Spenser, and Milton, but also the full range of African-American poetry (Williams, "Brooks's Way" 972).

If you mention the author's name or the title of the work in your paper, only a page reference is needed.

> According to Gladys Margaret Williams in "Gwendolyn Brooks's Way with the Sonnet," Brooks combines a sensitivity to poetic forms with a depth of emotion appropriate for her subject matter (972-73).

SAMPLE PARENTHETICAL REFERENCES

An entire work

> August Wilson's play *Fences* treats many themes frequently expressed in modern drama.

When citing an entire work, state the name of the author in your paper instead of in a parenthetical reference.

A work by two or three authors

> Myths cut across boundaries and cultural spheres and reappear in strikingly similar forms from country to country (Feldman and Richardson 124).

> The effect of a work of literature depends on the audience's predispositions that derive from membership in various social groups (Hovland, Janis, and Kelley 87).

A work by more than three authors

> Hawthorne's short stories frequently use a combination of allegorical and symbolic methods (Guerin et al. 91).

The abbreviation *et al.* is Latin for "and others."

A work in an anthology

> In his essay "Flat and Round Characters," E. M. Forster
> distinguishes between one-dimensional characters and those that
> are well developed (Stevick 223-31).

The parenthetical reference cites the anthology (edited by Stevick) that contains Forster's essay; full information about the anthology appears in the list of works cited.

A work with volume and page numbers

> Critics consider The Zoo Story to be one of Albee's best plays
> (Eagleton 2:17).

An indirect source

> Wagner observed that myth and history stood before him "with
> opposing claims" (qtd. in Winkler 10).

The abbreviation *qtd. in* ("quoted in") indicates that the quoted material was not taken from the original source.

A play with numbered lines

> "Give thy thoughts no tongue," says Polonius, "Nor any
> unproportioned thought his act" (*Ham.* 1.3.64-65).

The parentheses contain the act, scene, and line numbers (in arabic numerals), separated by periods. When included in parenthetical references, titles of the books of the Bible and well-known literary works are often abbreviated—*Gen.* for *Genesis* and *Ado* for *Much Ado about Nothing,* for example.

A poem

> "I muse my life-long hate, and without flinch / I bear it nobly
> as I live my part," says Claude McKay in his bitterly ironic poem
> "The White City" (lines 3-4).

Notice that a slash (/) is used to separate lines of poetry run in with the text. (The slash is preceded and followed by one space.) The parenthetical reference cites the lines quoted. Include the word *line* or *lines* for the first reference but just the numbers for subsequent references.

An electronic source

If you are citing a source from the Internet or from an online service to which your library subscribes, remember that these sources frequently do not contain page numbers. If the source uses paragraph, section, or screen numbers, use the abbreviation "par." "sec.," or the full word "screen."

> ```
> The earliest type of movie censoring came in the form of
> licensing fees, and in Deer River, Minnesota, "a licensing fee of
> $200 was deemed not excessive for a town of 1000" (Ernst, par.
> 20).
> ```

If the source has no page numbers or markers of any kind, cite the entire work. (When readers get to the works-cited list, they will be able to determine the nature of the source.)

> ```
> In her article "Limited Horizons," Lynne Cheney says that schools
> do best when students read literature not for what it tells them
> about the workplace, but for its insights into the human
> condition.
> ```

> ```
> Because of its parody of communism, the film Antz is actually an
> adult film masquerading as a child's tale (Clemin).
> ```

THE LIST OF WORKS CITED

Parenthetical references refer to a **works-cited list** that includes all the sources you refer to in your paper. Begin the works-cited list on a new page, continuing the page numbers of the paper. For example, if the text of the paper ends on page 6, the works-cited section will begin on page 7.

Informal Documentation

Sometimes, when you are writing a paper that includes quotations from a single source that the entire class has read, or if all your sources are from your textbook, your instructor may give you permission to use *informal documentation*. Because both the instructor and the class are familiar with the sources, you supply the authors' last names and page numbers in parentheses but do not include a works-cited list.

Center the title *Works Cited* one inch from the top of the page. Arrange entries alphabetically, according to the last name of each author. Use the first word of the title if the author is unknown (articles—*a, an,* and *the*—

at the beginning of a title are not considered first words). To conserve space, publishers' names are abbreviated—for example, *U. of California P* (for University of California Press). Double-space the entire works-cited list between and within entries. Begin typing each entry at the left margin, and indent subsequent lines five spaces (or one-half inch). Each works-cited entry has three divisions—author, title, and publishing information—separated by periods. The *MLA Handbook for Writers of Research Papers* shows a single space after all end punctuation.

Below is a directory of the sample entries that follow.

Entries for Books

1. A book by a single author

2. A book by two or three authors

3. A book by more than three authors

4. Two or more works by the same author

5. An edited book

6. A book with a volume number

7. A short story, poem, or play in a collection of the author's work

8. A short story in an anthology

9. A poem in an anthology

10. A play in an anthology

11. An article in an anthology

12. More than one selection from the same anthology

13. A translation

Entries for Articles

14. An article in a journal with continuous pagination throughout an annual volume

15. An article with separate pagination in each issue

16. An article in a magazine

17. An article in a daily newspaper

18. An article in a reference book

Entries for Other Sources

19. A film or videocassette
20. An interview
21. A lecture or an address

Entries for Electronic Sources (Internet)

22. A scholarly project or information database on the Internet
23. A document within a scholarly project or information database on the Internet
24. A personal site on the Internet
25. A book on the Internet
26. An article in a scholarly journal on the Internet
27. An article in an encyclopedia on the Internet
28. An article in a newspaper on the Internet
29. An article in a magazine on the Internet
30. A painting or photograph on the Internet
31. An e-mail
32. An online posting

Entries for Electronic Sources (Subscription Service)

33. A scholarly journal article with separate pagination in each issue from a subscription service
34. A scholarly journal article with continuous pagination throughout an annual volume from a subscription service
35. A monthly magazine article from a subscription service
36. A newspaper article from a subscription service
37. A reference book article from a subscription service
38. A dictionary definition from a subscription service

Entries for Other Electronic Sources

39. A nonperiodical publication on CD-ROM
40. A periodical publication on CD-ROM

Entries for Books

1. A book by a single author

Kingston, Maxine Hong. <u>The Woman Warrior: Memoirs of a Girlhood</u>
<u>among Ghosts</u>. New York: Knopf, 1976.

2. A book by two or three authors

Feldman, Burton, and Robert D. Richardson. <u>The Rise of Modern</u>
<u>Mythology</u>. Bloomington: Indiana UP, 1972.

Notice that only the *first* author's name is in reverse order.

3. A book by more than three authors

Guerin, Wilfred, et al., eds. <u>A Handbook of Critical Approaches</u>
<u>to Literature</u>. 3rd ed. New York: Harper, 1992.

Instead of using *et al.*, you may list all the authors' names in the order in which they appear on the title page.

4. Two or more works by the same author

Novoa, Juan-Bruce. <u>Chicano Authors: Inquiry by Interview</u>. Austin:
U of Texas P, 1980.
———. "Themes in Rudolfo Anaya's Work." Address given at New
Mexico State University, Las Cruces. 11 Apr. 1987.

List two or more works by the same author in alphabetical order by title. Include the author's full name in the first entry; use three unspaced hyphens followed by a period to take the place of the author's name in second and subsequent entries.

5. An edited book

Oosthuizen, Ann, ed. <u>Sometimes When It Rains: Writings by South</u>
<u>African Women</u>. New York: Pandora, 1987.

Notice that here the abbreviation *ed.* stands for *editor*.

6. A book with a volume number

When all the volumes of a multivolume work have the same title, list the number of the volume you used.

Eagleton, T. Allston. <u>A History of the New York Stage</u>. Vol. 2.
Englewood Cliffs: Prentice, 1987.

When each volume of a multivolume work has a separate title, list the title of the volume you used.

> Durant, Will, and Ariel Durant. <u>The Age of Napoleon: A History of
> European Civilization from 1789 to 1815</u>. New York: Simon,
> 1975.

The Age of Napoleon is volume 2 of *The Story of Civilization.* You need not provide information about the work as a whole.

7. *A short story, poem, or play in a collection of the author's work*

> Gordimer, Nadine. "Once upon a Time." <u>"Jump" and Other Stories</u>.
> New York: Farrar, 1991. 23-30.

8. *A short story in an anthology*

> Salinas, Marta. "The Scholarship Jacket." <u>Nosotros: Latina
> Literature Today</u>. Ed. Maria del Carmen Boza, Beverly Silva,
> and Carmen Valle. Binghamton: Bilingual, 1986. 68-70.

Note that here the abbreviation *Ed.* stands for *Edited by.* The inclusive page numbers follow the year of publication.

9. *A poem in an anthology*

> Simmerman, Jim. "Child's Grave, Hale County, Alabama." <u>The
> Pushcart Prize, X: Best of the Small Presses</u>. Ed. Bill
> Henderson. New York: Penguin, 1986. 198-99.

10. *A play in an anthology*

> Hughes, Langston. <u>Mother and Child. Black Drama Anthology</u>. Ed.
> Woodie King and Ron Miller. New York: NAL, 1986. 399-406.

11. *An article in an anthology*

> Forster, E. M. "Flat and Round Characters." <u>The Theory of the
> Novel</u>. Ed. Philip Stevick. New York: Free, 1980. 223-31.

12. *More than one selection from the same anthology*

If you are using more than one selection from an anthology, cite the anthology in a separate entry. Then, list each individual selection separately, including the author and title of the selection, the anthology editor's last name, and the inclusive page numbers.

Baxter, Charles. "Gryphon." Kirszner and Mandell 136-47.
Kirszner, Laurie G., and Stephen R. Mandell, eds. Literature:
    Reading, Reacting, Writing. 5th ed. Boston: Wadsworth, 2004.
Rich, Adrienne. "Diving into the Wreck." Kirszner and Mandell
    1019-21.

13. A translation

Carpentier, Alejo. Reasons of State. Trans. Francis Partridge.
    New York: Norton, 1976.

Entries for Articles

Article citations include the author's name; the title of the article (in quotation marks); the name of the periodical (underlined); and the pages on which the full article appears (without the abbreviations *p.* or *pp.*).

14. An article in a journal with continuous pagination throughout an annual volume

LeGuin, Ursula K. "American Science Fiction and the Other."
    Science Fiction Studies 2 (1975): 208-10.

15. An article with separate pagination in each issue

Grossman, Robert. "The Grotesque in Faulkner's 'A Rose for
    Emily.'" Mosaic 20.3 (1987): 40-55.

Note that *20.3* signifies volume 20, issue 3.

16. An article in a magazine

Milosz, Czeslaw. "A Lecture." The New Yorker 22 June 1992: 32.
"Solzhenitsyn: An Artist Becomes an Exile." Time 25 Feb. 1974:
    34+.

Note that 34+ indicates that the article appears on pages that are not consecutive; in this case, the article begins on page 34 and continues on page 37. An article with no listed author is entered by title on the works-cited list.

17. An article in a daily newspaper

Oates, Joyce Carol. "When Characters from the Page Are Made Flesh
    on the Screen." New York Times 23 Mar. 1986, late ed.: C1+.

C1+ indicates that the article begins on page 1 of Section C and continues on a subsequent page.

18. *An article in a reference book*

Do not include publication information for well-known reference books.

> "Dance Theatre of Harlem." The New Encyclopaedia Britannica:
> Micropaedia. 15th ed. 1987.

Include publication information when citing reference books that are not well known.

> Grimstead, David. "Fuller, Margaret Sarah." Encyclopedia of
> American Biography. Ed. John A. Garraty. New York: Harper,
> 1974.

Entries for Other Sources

19. *A film or videocassette*

> "A Worn Path." By Eudora Welty. Dir. John Reid and Claudia
> Velasco. Perf. Cora Lee Day and Conchita Ferrell.
> Videocassette. Wadsworth, 1994.

20. *An interview*

> Brooks, Gwendolyn. "An Interview with Gwendolyn Brooks."
> Triquarterly 60 (1984): 405-10.

21. *A lecture or an address*

> Novoa, Juan-Bruce. "Themes in Rudolfo Anaya's Work." Literature
> Colloquium. New Mexico State University. Las Cruces. 11 Apr.
> 1987.

Entries for Electronic Sources (Internet)

MLA style recognizes relevant publication information is not always available for electronic sources. Include in your citation whatever information you can reasonably obtain. Include both the date of the electronic publication (if available) and the date you accessed the source. In addition, include the URL (electronic address) in angle brackets. If you have to carry the URL over to the next line, divide it after a slash. If the URL is excessively long, use just the URL of the site's search page, or use the URL of the site's home page, followed by the word *path* and a colon and then the sequence of links to follow.

22. *A scholarly project or information database on the Internet*

Philadelphia Writers Project. Ed. Miriam Kotzen Green. May 1998.
Drexel U. 12 June 1999 <http://www.Drexel.edu/letrs/wwp/>.

23. *A document within a scholarly project or information database on the Internet*

"D-Day: June 7th, 1944." The History Channel Online. 1999.
History Channel. 7 June 1999 <http://historychannel.com/
thisday/today/997690.html>.

24. *A personal site on the Internet*

Yerkes, James. Chiron's Forum: John Updike Home Page. 23 June
1999. 30 June 1999 <http://www.users.fast.net/~joyerkers/
item9.html>.

25. *A book on the Internet*

Douglass, Frederick. My Bondage and My Freedom. Boston: 1855. 8
June 1999 <gopher://gopher.vt.edu:10024/22/178/3>.

26. *An article in a scholarly journal on the Internet*

Dekoven, Marianne. "Utopias Limited: Post-Sixties and Postmodern
American Fiction." Modern Fiction Studies 41.1 (1995): 13 pp.
17 Mar. 1999 <http://muse.jhu.edu/journals/mfs.v041/
41.1dwkovwn.html>.

When you cite information from the print version of an electronic source,
include the publication information for the printed source, the number of
pages or paragraphs (if available), and the date of access.

27. *An article in an encyclopedia on the Internet*

"Hawthorne, Nathaniel." Britannica Online. Vers. 98.2. Apr. 1998.
Encyclopedia Britannica. 16 May 1998 <http://www.eb/com/
:220>.

28. *An article in a newspaper on the Internet*

Lohr, Steve. "Microsoft Goes to Court." New York Times on the Web
19 Oct. 1998. 29 Apr. 1999 <http://www.nytimes.com/web/
docroot/library.cyber/week/1019business.html>.

29. *An article in a magazine on the Internet*

> Weiser, Jay. "The Tyranny of Informality." Time 26 Feb. 1996.
>   1 Mar. 1999 <http://www.enews.com/magazines.tnr/current/
>   022696.3.html>.

30. *A painting or photograph on the Internet*

> Lange, Dorothea, <u>Looking at Pictures</u>. 1936. Museum of Mod. Art,
>   New York. 17 July 2000 <http://moma.org/exhibitions/
>   lookingatphotographs/lang-fr.html>.

31. *An e-mail*

> Adkins, Camille. E-mail to the author. 28 June 2001.

32. *An online posting*

> Gilford, Mary. "Dog Heroes in Children's Literature." Online
>   posting. 17 Mar. 1999. 12 Apr. 1999 <news:alt.animals.dogs>.

Entries for Electronic Sources (Online Subscription Service)

Online subscription services can be divided into those you subscribe to, such as America Online, and those that your college library subscribes to, such as Extended Academic ASAP, Lexis-Nexis, and ProQuest Direct.

To cite information from an online service to which you subscribe, you have two options. If the service provides a URL, follow the examples in entries 22 through 30. If the service enables you to use a keyword to access material, provide the keyword (following the date of access) at the end of the entry.

> "Kafka, Franz." <u>Compton's Encyclopedia Online</u>. Vers. 3.0. 2000.
>   America Online. 8 June 2001. Keyword: Compton's.

If, instead of a keyword, you follow a series of topic labels, list them (separated by semicolons) after the word *Path*.

> "Elizabeth Adams." <u>History Resources</u>. 11 Nov. 2001. America
>   Online. 28 Apr. 2001. Path: Research; Biology; Women in
>   Science; Biographies.

To cite information from an online service to which your library subscribes, include the underlined name of the database (if known), the name
of the service, the library, the date of access, and the URL of the online
service's home page.

> Luckenbill, Trent. "Environmental Litigation: Down the Endless
> Corridor." Environment 17 July 2001: 34-42. ABI/INFORM
> GLOBAL. ProQuest Direct. Drexel U Lib., Philadelphia. 12 Oct.
> 2001 <http://www.umi.com/proquest>.

33. *A scholarly journal article with separate pagination in each issue
from an online service*

> Schaefer, Richard J. "Editing Strategies in Television News
> Documentaries." Journal of Communication 47.4 (1997): 69-89.
> InfoTrac OneFile Plus. Gale Group Databases. Augusta R.
> Kolwyck Lib., Chattanooga, TN. 2 Oct. 2002 <http://
> library.cstcc.cc.tn.us/ref3.shtml>.

34. *A scholarly journal article with continuous pagination throughout
an annual volume from an online service*

> Hudson, Nicholas. "Samuel Johnson, Urban Culture, and the
> Geography of Postfire London." Studies in English Literature
> 42 (2002): 557-80. MasterFILE Premier. EBSCOhost. Augusta R.
> Kolwyck Lib., Chattanooga, TN. 2 Oct. 2002 <http://
> library.cstcc.cc.tn.us/ref3.shtml>.

35. *A monthly magazine article from an online service*

> Livermore, Beth. "Meteorites on Ice." Astronomy July 1993: 54-58.
> Expanded Academic ASAP Plus. Gale Group Databases. Augusta R.
> Kolwyck Lib., Chattanooga, TN. 2 Oct. 2002 <http://
> library.cstcc.cc.tn.us/ref3.shtml>.

36. *A newspaper article from an online service*

> Meyer, Greg. "Answering Questions about the West Nile Virus."
> Dayton Daily News 11 July 2002: Z3-Z7. LexisNexis Academic.
> Augusta R. Kolwyck Lib., Chattanooga, TN. 2 Oct. 2002
> <http://library.cstcc.cc.tn.us/ref3.shtml>.

37. *A reference book article from an online service*

> Laird, Judith. "Geoffrey Chaucer." Cyclopedia of World Authors.
> 1997. MagillOnLiterature. EBSCOhost. Augusta R. Kolwyck Lib.,

Chattanooga, TN. 2 Oct. 2002 <http://library.cstcc.cc.tn.us/
ref3.shtml>.

38. *A dictionary definition from an online service*

"Migraine." <u>Mosby's Medical, Nursing, and Allied Health
Dictionary</u>. 1998 ed. <u>Health Reference Center</u>. Gale Group
Databases. Augusta R. Kolwyck Lib., Chattanooga, TN. 2 Oct.
2002 <http://library.cstcc.cc.tn.us/ref3.shtml>.

Entries for Other Electronic Sources

39. *A nonperiodical publication on CD-ROM*

"Windhover." <u>The Oxford English Dictionary</u>. 2nd ed. CD-ROM.
Oxford: Oxford UP, 1992.

40. *A periodical publication on CD-ROM*

Zurbach, Kate. "The Linguistic Roots of Three Terms." <u>Linguistic
Quarterly</u> 37 (1994): 12-47. <u>InfoTrac: Magazine Index Plus</u>.
CD-ROM. Information Access. Jan. 1996.

WARNING: Using information from an Internet source can be risky.
Contributors are not necessarily experts, and they frequently are inaccu-
rate or misinformed. Unless you can be certain that the information you
are obtaining from these sources is reliable, do not use it. You can check
the reliability of an Internet source by asking your instructor or librarian
for guidance.

CONTENT NOTES

Use **content notes,** indicated by a superscript (a raised number) in the
text, to cite several sources at once or to provide commentary or explana-
tions that do not fit smoothly into your paper. The full text of these notes
appears on the first numbered page following the last page of the paper.
(If your paper has no content notes, the works-cited page follows the last
page of the paper.) Like works-cited entries, content notes are double-
spaced within and between entries. However, the first line of each
explanatory note is indented five spaces (or one-half inch), and subsequent lines are flush with the left-hand margin.

To Cite Several Sources

In the paper

Surprising as it may seem, there have been many attempts to define literature.[1]

In the note

[1] For an overview of critical opinion, see Arnold 72; Eagleton 1-2; Howe 43-44; and Abrams 232-34.

To Provide Explanations

In the paper

In recent years, gothic novels have achieved great popularity.[3]

In the note

[3] Gothic novels, works written in imitation of medieval romances, originally relied on supernatural occurrences. They flourished in the late eighteenth and early nineteenth centuries.

Text Credits

Alkalay-Gut, Karen. "Murder and Marriage: Another Look at *Trifles*." From Susan Glaspell: Essay on Her Theater and Fiction © 1995 The University of Michigan Press. Reprinted by permission of The University of Michigan Press.

Ben-Zvi, Linda. "Murder, She Wrote: The Genesis of Susan Glaspell's *Trifles*." Theatre Journal 44:2 (1992): 141–162. © The Johns Hopkins University Press. Reprinted with permission of The Johns Hopkins University Press.

Mael, Phyllis. "*Trifles*: The Path to Sisterhood" Literature/Film Quarterly 17.4 (1989): 281–284. © Literature/Film Quarterly/Salisbury University. Reprinted by permission of Literature/Film Quarterly.

Mustazza, Leonard. "Generic Translation and Thematic Shift in Susan Glaspell's *Trifles* and 'A Jury of Her Peers'" Studies in Short Fiction 26.4 (1989): 489–496. © 1989 Studies in Short Fiction, Inc.

Stein, Karen F. "The Women's World of Glaspell's *Trifles*" from Women in American Theatre, Helen Krich Chinoy/Linda Walsh Jenkins, eds. © 1981. Reprinted by permission of the author.

Photo Credits

Page 13, Susan Glaspell: © AP/Wide World Photos

Page 14, Provincetown Playhouse: © Bettmann/CORBIS.

Page 45, Production of *Trifles*: © Billy Rose Theatre Collection, New York Public Library for the Performing Arts. Astor, Lenox, and Tilden Foundation.